Love is
Not Enough

Changing Dysfunctional Family Habits

David W. Earle, LPC

Picphotos.net generously provided the
Black Background Art Wallpaper for the
front cover free of change. I am indebted
for their kindness.

Books coauthored by the same author

- *Leadership – Helping others to Succeed –*
    Senator George Mitchell, Patricia Schroeder, et al
- *Extreme Excellence –*
    Michael Higson, Arlene R. Taylor, et al

Other books by the same author

- *What To Do While You Count To 10*
- *Professor of Pain*
- *Iron Mask*
- *Red Roses 'n Pinstripes*
- *Gilligan's Notes*
- *Wisdom of the Twelve Steps* – Workbook Step I
- *Wisdom of the Twelve Steps* – Workbook Step II
- *Wisdom of the Twelve Steps* – Workbook Step III
- *Wisdom of the Twelve Steps* – Workbook Step IV
- *Wisdom of the Twelve Steps* – Workbook Step V
- *Wisdom of the Twelve Steps* – Workbook Step VI
- *Wisdom of the Twelve Steps* – Workbook Step XI
- *Wisdom of the Twelve Steps* – Workbook Step XII

ISBN-13: 978-1499228915
ISBN-10: 1499228910

The human spirit" can recover and heal.
It takes patience, gut level sharing
with family and friends,
research, and lots of soul searching. "
Sharon Cruse

Table of Contents

Introduction

*"The only person you are destined
to become is the person
you decide to be. "*
Ralph Waldo Emerson

How did you learn to ride a bicycle? By falling off, right? One woman told me she never learned how to ride a bicycle. Surprised, I asked her, "Didn't someone run alongside of you holding onto the seat and then let go for you to learn to balance the bike?"

"Oh, yes," she told me. "My daddy did."

I was confused. "Then how come you cannot ride a bike?" I asked.

She smiled weakly, "My daddy never would let go."

In order to learn, we have to let go of what we know and accept that we will suffer the inevitable falls with their cuts, bruises, and occasional broken bones with accompanying pain. This is the price of our journey's ticket. Success requires getting back on the bike after our fall and trying to ride again and again. Many want to ride a bicycle but not everyone is willing to pay the price to learn. Victory belongs to us when our perseverance pays off and we can loudly exclaim, "Look at me, Daddy!" as we show off our hard won achievement.

"What is the object of education?" This question I posed to my students when I taught at the University of Phoenix. Their responses were probably similar to yours, such as being educated, obtaining knowledge, changing jobs, or with some students only a shoulder-shrug of indifference. These are typical reactions to this question but consider this definition: *the object of education is to unlearn.*

Unlearn, what do you mean? When you first entered that scary high school geometry class, you probably had some inkling of what the course entailed stemming from all the horror stories told by upperclassmen, the prediction of failure proclaimed by your big sister, and your own worries and anxieties. After you completed geometry and breathed the sigh of relief from having passed this course, your understanding of geometry was completely different than what you thought when class began. Finishing high school geometry, you were now "unlearned". This unlearning experience increased your education.

Most people have an understanding about how they were raised, how they cope with life, and how to love. After you finish this book you will "unlearn" information concerning these topics. This education will be much more valuable than the cost of this book or the time invested in reading it. Habits become rails where we ride our trains of life. *Love Is Not Enough* teaches habits that provide a chance to step back from our rails, view ourselves and others from a different perspective, and see if these rails are going toward or away from our goals.

Are you ready to change? Maybe a better question is...are you ready to fall off the bicycle? As strange as these questions may seem, determining if you are ready to change is an important question to ask yourself, remember...change always exacts a price. You may want a calm and peaceful life, but if the price of change is too great, if you are unwilling to break destructive habits, or you are too comfortable with your old companion – *Master Misery* - nothing will happen.

Nothing will happen if your chaos is more dominant than your desire to change. Nothing will happen if your pervasive resistance locks you in status quo. Without struggle...*nothing will happen*. Without struggle...chaos will ultimately trump your desire for peace and serenity. Without struggle...nothing will happen. You must take the first step.

Are you ready to struggle? Are you ready to change?

I loved my family very much and gave them all the love I knew how to give and I operated with what I knew best. The dysfunctional habits you read about in this book are the same ones that I raised my family with; it was the roadmap I learned growing up and used to express the love I felt. As one of my clients told me about her dysfunctional family, "...came from one...made one." She told me being dysfunctional became a joke in her family and her family's answering machine messages stated, "Greeting, you have reached the dysfunctional family of..."

> *"...everyone wants to live on top of the mountain,*
> *but all the happiness and growth occurs*
> *while you're climbing it."*
> Andy Rooney

With a similar set of dysfunctional principles as my guide, my love often came out sideways and caused pain instead of what I intended. Try as I might, *my love was not working!* Until I learned new and functional ways of expressing love, my loved ones did not receive what I truly wanted to give, what they wanted, and what they deserved to receive. After unlearning my learned dysfunction, I now know… *love was not enough.*

Allow the pain from your dysfunctional lifestyle to fuel this change process; the energy of your past pain can sustain your change. If you do not allow the pain to guide you and be your source of inspiration, this book will find itself on the shelf with the other unread self-help books collecting dust and patiently awaiting your return. You will miss this opportunity to unlearn.

Change is scary. Change requires stepping out into the darkness of the unknown, leaving the comfort of the familiar, the known. All this book can do is shine a light on the path ahead but the darkness will still cast shadows over this path. You will be the one who steps out beyond the light, trusting there is solid ground beneath you. Pain can be your flashlight if you allow it's bright beam to show you the way. You have already paid the price for this flashlight; why not use it?

Love Is Not Enough will help you discover who *you really are* by discovering and claiming the wonderful world of you. From confusion comes clarity. Embrace the uncertainty. Hug the doubt. It is okay to not have all the answers and be willing to unlearn.

"Scars have the strange power to
remind us that our past is real."
Cormac McCarthy

Promise

In the TV Sitcom *The Big Bang Theory*, one of the characters, Sheldon Cooper, doesn't know how to relate to other people. Although he lacks coping skills, he's learned an important one…to offer someone in distress, "a cup of hot beverage." I want to look you in the eye, offer you a hot beverage, and make a promise.

I'd like your permission to be blunt. Do I have it? Okay, here it is. You chose this book because something in your life is not quite working, as you would like. Rarely do we pick up a self-help book when everything is okay. You have an unsettling feeling that something is missing and life is not as you wish. My bluntness says, "Good." Your restlessness propelled you to open this book and begin reading. Allow your discontent to provide the energy and courage you need to complete the arduous but delightful task of self-understanding and personal acceptance.

Now for my promise: read this simple, relatively short book. Work the exercises, thinking them through and write about each of the questions. There is something very revealing and almost magical in honest reflection expressed on paper then periodically reread. The explorer gains considerable wisdom when combining reading the narrative, answering the questions, then in a quiet mind, honestly reflecting upon what they wrote.

Do all of these things and your life will be better. From my experience of changing me (probably a lot harder job that you will have with you), and thousands of mental health clients I've worked with over twenty plus years, I promise your life will be richer, happier, and you will be thankful for this process.

You will be able to share your great love now begging for a more profound expression. You will be happier, your significant others will be happier, and life will be sweeter. This is my promise. Enjoy your hot beverage.

Reasons *NOT* to read

- **Don't read *Love Is Not Enough* if you are not ready to change.**

- **Don't read this book if you are not willing to work the**
- **exercises.**

- **Don't read this book if you are too comfortable in your current life and want to stay in status quo.**

- **Don't read this book if you are not willing to pay the price change requires.**

Are these scary realizations? Yes, they are but do not worry. If you are still reading, you have something going for you. You are unique. Those questions scare many away. You, however, already have the necessary courage to make the changes in your life. You can achieve any goal you set your mind to accomplish. If there was real doubt, you would not have chosen this book to explore, or after reading the "don't statements" above, you would have discarded this book like yesterday's newspaper.

When I first entered the family treatment part of the chemical dependency program at the hospital where my son was a patient, they gave me a book called the *12x12*. This thin book explained the *Twelve Steps and Twelve Traditions of Alcoholics Anonymous*. As instructed, I went home and dutifully read the book, front to back.

When I finished it, I was so mad I threw it across the room. I have a very vivid memory of seeing this small book sailing through the air with its pages opening like wings as it smashed into the fireplace. I remember saying aloud, "That is a bunch of &%$!&. Nothing could be that simple! This can never work!" You may be like me and need to hurl this book across the room, for the principles listed here are simple, perhaps too simple for complicated people, but they have worked and for countless others...*they will work for you.*

There are certain lessons everyone must learn to have a successful life. What are the lessons you must know? Try this tongue twister. You see, your *knower* knows what you need to know. You may not know that your *knower* knows, but, believe me, your *knower* knows – just trust your *knower* to know what you need to know.

It is up to you when or *if* you choose to learn these lessons. Some people stick their foot into the change process; they obtain a little healing, then for some reason they stop. Some of my mental health clients make a few sessions, discover some insights, and choose not to return. I once encouraged a young man to attend an Adult Children of Alcoholics meeting. After his first meeting, he told me how much he loved it and proudly exclaimed, "This is my meeting. I got so much out of it."

I was so happy for him but, strangely, he never went back. Think about his decision. Here was a resource he recognized as being a valuable tool in his search for happiness, but instead of attending, he went back to his old behavior – what he knew best. I sometimes think of how his life would have been different if he had chosen to learn those lessons then, instead of waiting and paying a higher and higher price for his discontent and lack of action.

This book is for those who want to change. It is not for the weak, for it involves actively thinking about how your parents raised you and what you now want for you and your family. Questioning why your parents raised you in dysfunction is not a productive question. Your childhood has already happened and you cannot change it. Asking *why* this happened is a poor question if progress is your goal. A better approach is, "Okay, this happened to me but now it is up to me to decide what I am going to do about it."

This book is not about bashing families. Despite the pain you endured as a child – from a little to excessive amounts - most parents did the best they could and gave their children everything they knew how to give. Like it or not, these behaviors are your heritage; they were passed down to your parents from their parents and, ultimately, inflicted upon you. This realization helps in accepting your parents as fallible human beings, not the all-knowing and all-powerful beings you once thought they were. You will come to see them as vulnerable, wounded, and in their own pain. They unintentionally inflicted their pain upon you, their child. Your wounds are the byproduct of their ignorance. Knowing this helps in the forgiveness process, and if your parents are like me, they ardently desire forgiveness from their offspring but are limited in obtaining forgiveness without the understanding of their children.

"Obstacles are those frightful things you see when you take your eyes off the goal."
Henry Ford

Six Parts of Love is Not Enough:

Part I – When Chaos is Normal

Using a model entitled "Family Sculpturing-Dysfunctional Families," families are dissected into the various dysfunctional roles family members tend to adopt.

> *"I am not a product of my circumstances.*
> *I am a product of my decisions."*
> Stephen Covey

Part II – Family Sculpturing

Families often adopt various family roles to express the pain living in dysfunctional families.

> *"...people will forget what you said,*
> *people will forget what you did,*
> *but people will never forget how*
> *you made them feel."*
> Maya Angelou

Part III – Dysfunctional Family Habits

Dysfunctional families develop certain love-limiting habits that become the centerpiece of how family members relate to one another.

> *"The Universe operates on a basic principle of economics: everything*
> *has its cost. We pay to create our future, we pay for the mistakes*
> *of the past. We pay for every change we make*
> *and we pay just as dearly if we refuse to change."*
> Brian Herbert

Part IV – The Truth Is...

This section has three parts and is based upon a powerful essay. This essay first defines the problem, then discusses the solution, and ends with emphasizing forgiveness.

> *"Whether you think you can*
> *or you think you can't...*
> *you are right."*
> Henry Ford

Part V – Dysfunctional Family Habits Antidotes

After reading about these habits, the reader may exclaim, "Now what? I have these habits, but what do I do?" This section is the answer to "Now what?" where antidotes to these dysfunctional habits are taught.

> *"If you hear a voice within you saying,*
> *you cannot paint, then by all means paint*
> *and that voice will be silenced.*
> Vincent Van Gogh

Part VI – Relapse

On your journey through self-discovery and change, I promise you will fail; it's part of the struggle. Upon failing, you have the choice to pick yourself up off the canvas, dust yourself off and begin again, having now learned another powerful lesson. Maybe you will choose to return to the dysfunctions you know so well, or let them go in favor of something much more powerful allowing a richer and fuller ability to love. *Your* choice.

> *"The best revenge is massive success."*
> Frank Sinatra

Note: There are 52 active exercises throughout this book and I encourage you to spend time reflecting on each question. In this manner, the lessons presented become active accomplishments instead of cold, textbook facts that may sound good when read but will not have the impact necessary for change until you actively experience them.

> *"Tell me and I forget,*
> *teach me and I may remember,*
> *involve me and I learn."*
> Benjamin Franklin

Part I – When Chaos is Normal

*"Life is nothing without a little chaos
to make it interesting."*
Amelia Atwater-Rhodes

All families have some degree of chaos, from a little to a lot. Whatever the amount experienced, this degree-no matter how painful-becomes normal...*your normal*. Chaos is what we know best. Having this chaos then becomes our way to relate to the world; it becomes our "Chaos Habit". Having these habits, you are often unaware of this unpleasant fact and not conscious of how these patterns affect your life. You don't know how you allowed the dysfunction of chaos to become your self-definition. Although not on a conscious level, when turmoil is ever-present family chaos becomes our personal self-definition.

If you grew up in chaos, serenity – an inner sense of calm – can seem abnormal, like a distant goal that is elusive yet so tantalizingly close. When we "chaos people" find ourselves experiencing a wonderful state of temporary happiness, it feels contrary to what we know best and then confusion sets in. Since Chaos People are uncomfortable with peace-we return to dysfunction-the chaos we grew up with and know best. We do not know ourselves without our constant companion, chaos, and only have fleeting glimpses of experiencing ourselves in a peaceful state.

However, it is not until the chaos becomes so great, so powerful, so painful do we decide to change and become willing to struggle. This decision creates a great deal of uncertainty and confusion. Who will we become as we struggle to escape the dysfunction morass? If this describes you, this book will help define the habits of dysfunctional families. After reading it, you will recognize many of the habits are alive today just as you learned them growing up and since they were so common, family members viewed them as normal.

Giving up the habits we learned living in chaos will be difficult but is the price we must pay for peace and serenity. Logically, we ask ourselves, "Why would anyone want to live in chaos?" Good question, but often we do. If chaos is normal for you, change toward peace and serenity is abnormal. Changing to a peaceful life, however desirable, is difficult, for it requires altering lifelong habits of thinking and behaving. The change from dysfunction to peace is not easy and often painful, but when you finally discard these habits and find yourself on the other side, you too will find your peace, your serenity, and your tranquility.

Actually, peace and serenity is the natural state of existence and is your birthright. Peace and serenity are your inheritance and it is up to you to claim what is yours. Claiming this state of calmness, serenity, and joy requires a fight to change self-definition, habits of thinking, and coping skills. It requires going inside of you, finding, and claiming your birth inheritance, an internal sense of joy, happiness, serenity, and the comfortable feeling of being okay. These gifts are yours. When growing up in chaos and perpetuating this chaos as adults, we give away the natural state of serenity. The question is not why we give it away, but how to get it back. With this new awareness, this "how" to reclaim what is rightfully ours becomes the focus of the beautiful inward journey and this book provides a reliable roadmap for this change.

Even those who ~~have~~ have achieved this elusive state of peace and serenity, their natural state, are subjected to the stress of life. When trauma and stress occur, people often retreat to what they know, their normal: chaos. Under stressful conditions, no matter how wonderful peace and serenity are, chaos people tend to revert to old behaviors, resulting in the same destructive thinking and behaving they swore never to do again. They have fallen off their bicycle.

Once the peaceful state becomes their new normal, falling backwards into chaos becomes so abhorrent, so much in contrast, they struggle to divorce chaos and return to peace. However, on the inward trail toward self-discovery, relapse happens and again they fall off the bicycle. Often, this falling is the learning necessary to realize where they really want to be. The best learning often comes from these relapses and as uncomfortable as the slip may be, it is a necessary part of learning. When you fall are you determined to get back on your bicycle?

> *"Definiteness of purpose is the starting*
> *point of all achievement."*
> W. Clement

As you read about dysfunctional families, you may be tempted to explain away what you experienced, justify your upbringing, rationalize away what hurts, or explain why your family was different. These are all natural reactions and your family probably *is* different from some described in this book. What I encourage you to do is not to judge how you were raised in terms of bad or good, but rather look for areas where your family was similar to these concepts. Seek this understanding with the intention of improving yours and subsequent generations, so you can pass back what doesn't work and pass on to others and especially your loved ones new and better methods of communicating love..

> *To love life, to love it even when you have no stomach for it*
> *and everything you've held dear crumbles*
> *like burnt paper in your hands,*
> *your throat filled with the silt of it.*
> *When grief sits with you,*
> *its tropical heat thickens the air,*
> *heavy as water more fit for gills than lungs,*
> *when grief weights you like your own flesh only more of it,*
> *an obesity of grief, you think,*
> *how can your body withstand this?*
> *Then you hold life like a face between your palms,*
> *a plain face, no charming smile,*
> *no violet eyes, and you say,*
> *yes, I will take you, I will love again."*
> Ellen Bass

Comedian Jeff Foxworthy has a comic style that uses the set-up: "You might be a redneck if….". As a survivor of a chaos lifestyle, I can poke fun at you because, just as Jeff Foxworthy acknowledges his redneck heritage, I am also a chaos person. Happy people enjoy poking fun at themselves, so using Jeff's style, here is some comic relief and we'll share a few more as we continue this journey.

> ***You might be a Chaos Person if...***
> you use Sheldon Cooper
> from the TV Sitcom
> *The Big Bang Theory* as
> your personal life coach

Chaos Behaviour Club

Join this most Expensive Club – *See if you qualify.*

Club Benefits:
- Unlimited supply of anger
- Stress related diseases available to all members
- Isolation from others – even in a crowd
- Unable to express the love you feel – except destructively
- Personal needs will never be met
- No limit on emotional pain
- Living on the roller coaster called *Chaos*
- A haunting feeling that something is missing

Club Rules:
- Personal feelings can NEVER be expressed
- Everyone MUST have at least ONE compulsive behavior (The Rules Committee will have the final authority on the acceptability of each behavior submitted.)
- Love CANNOT be expressed – (except destructively)
- The ILLUSION of happiness must be maintained to all those outside the family-after all we must always look good
- No one can talk about their PAIN.
- No one can fully trust other people.

Membership Dues:
You must be willing to give up the following:
- Personal Peace
- Serenity
- Feeling Close to your Creator
- Feelings of Self–worth
- Any Feelings of "I'm OK"
- Self–love (no self-love allowed - absolute requirement)

Join NOW and avoid the rush! **Don't delay!**
(Most of your friends have already joined!)

Trait Continuum

There are many continuums in life where each end of the continuum represents an extreme. For example, the workaholic is on one end, and on the other end of the work continuum is the lazy bum who will not lift a finger. Visualize a person overeating themselves to death on one end and the bulimic starving to death on the other. Consider the over-involved, chatty-busybody person on one end and the silent hermit on the other both representing extreme ends of the same continuum.

Look at the diagram on the next page and read the various examples of extreme behaviors. There are many continuums in life; these represent only a few. Life is about balance and when living between the two extremes, when life is in balance...peace is the reward. However at either end of a continuum, there is chaos.

If you find yourself on one end of a continuum, do not be discouraged for it could be surprisingly one of your areas of personal strength. Strengths? Yes, some strength was issued at birth and some you developed as you matured. Many of your perceived weaknesses are really your strengths turned against you. Someone said, "Any strength when over-used becomes a weakness." If you are at one end or the other of any continuum, you are not a bad person but you may want to check to see if your strength may be working against you.

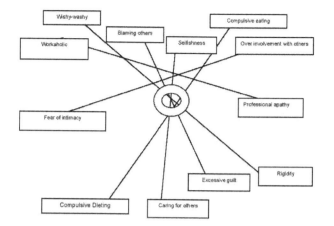

The actual author of this model is unknown, however, many other people have discussed these traits in their work such as: Gordon Allpot, Henry Murry, and Raymond Cattell

"Life ... will all balance out if you are attuned to what sustains your body and spirit."
Gina Shaw

Daredevil Nik Wallenda was the first man to cross Niagara Falls on a tightrope in 2012. He had a 30-foot pole and was constantly moving or adjusting to maintain his balance. Actually, he was always out of balance and the pole's movement was his physical correction to being imbalanced. Life is like this high-wire daredevil; successful living is between the two extremes. When life is out-of-balance, there is chaos. Think about this tightrope walker the next time you feel your life may be out of balance.

Now, again look at the Trait Diagram, but let your eye focus on the middle of the illustration. You'll notice on this diagram, the inner circle is not quite in the center. This is a graphic representation of living in the middle but, like the drawing, we are always somewhat out of balance. Like the tightrope walker, we constantly are required to find a balance between two diametrically opposed extremes. Finding and maintaining this balance is one of the significant struggles in life.

Exercise 1

Look at the various extremes, do you see yourself? Where?

Family Extremes

*"Without a filter,
a man is just chaos walking."*
Patrick Ness

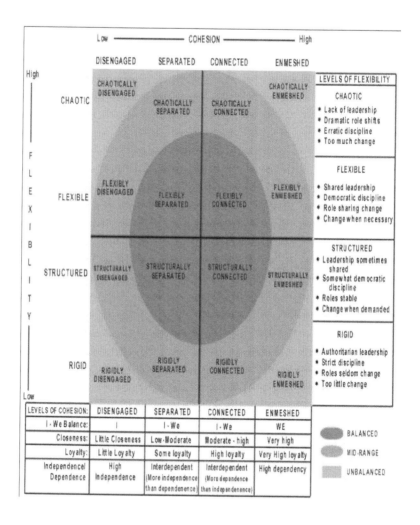

The *Circumplex Model of Family System* is another example high-lighting what happens when families or couples live in continuum-extremes. Drs. David H. Olson, Douglas Sprenkle and Candyce Russell developed the *Circumplex Mode,* a very useful diagnosis tool to study families. It has three dimensions that have repeatedly proven significant to understanding family dynamics. The three dimensions described in the Circumplex Model are *Cohesion, Flexibility,* and *Communication.* David H. Olson, Ph. D. graciously gave permission to use this model and provided suggestions on how best to show how these dynamics affects the free flow of love in families and couples.

Circumplex Model of Family Systems

"The Circumplex Model of Marital and Family systems was developed in an attempt to bridge the gap that typically exists between research, theory and practice (Olson, Russell and Sprenkle, 1979 & 1989)." This model measures the levels of family functioning on two different continuums: **Cohesion** on the horizontal axis and **Flexibility** on the vertical. How families communicate is the third element to understanding family dynamics. Together these three elements help explain the dynamics of close relationships.

You notice on the diagram that this model has two continuums: the vertical axis is Flexibility and the Horizontal axis is Cohesion.

Flexibility is the vertical continuum with end of the axis represents a high degree and the opposite end is low. The greater the extreme direction, the more likely the family difficulties increase. The interaction of these two dynamics demonstrates the family effectiveness. Families finding themselves in either extreme gain increased effectiveness when moving toward the center.

Flexibility concerns how a family changes between the two ends of this continuum: rigidity at the low end versus chaos at the high end. The *Flexibility* axis measures the balance between stability vs. change. Families exhibiting high levels tend to be chaotic and families on the low levels tend to be rigid. Both extremes have increased problems, such as sadness and unhappiness.

Cohesion measures the family emotional connection. Families at the low end are disengaged and families at the high end experience enmeshment. *Cohesion* is the balance between separateness vs. togetherness; it measures the degree of family control. Families at one extreme of this measurement are rigid where one individual is very controlling, has the power, and is in charge. On the other end, there is little family leadership and what is there tends to be erratic and impulsive. Here communication is often unclear, not thought out, and confusing and the roles in this family are unclear and often shift from one individual to another. Blurred boundaries occur when one member has difficulty separating themselves from one another. Highly enmeshed or heavily disengaged families are problematic.

> The cute guy next to you
> has just been released from
> prison for killing his wife.
> *You might be a Chaos Person if...*
> you get interested and say,
> "So, you're single?"

Describing the *Flexibility* Extreme Ends:

Rigidly – In this family, there are rules, traditions, and absolute standards with which family members must comply. When a problem arises, one solution is to create a new rule. Family members know exactly what role they are to play, and woe be it for someone in this family to change: "This is the way our family does it, we've always done it this way, and by God we will honor these time-tested traditions!" *Cold* and *distant* are often the descriptive words for these families.

Chaotically – Rules and expectations constantly change in this type of family, often on a parental whim; leadership is erratic or very limited. There is very little structure and children can push parents around and take control of the family. Children pushing parents too far often result in sudden parental over-reaction and corresponding explosion. Decisions are often impulsive, not thought out, and often loaded with unmanaged and unintentional emotions and consequences. There are little if any clearly defined rules; what is in place can suddenly change. Children see structure as love, and in this type of family, there is little structure and *children do not feel loved.*

23

Describing the *Cohesion* Extreme Ends:

Disengaged – In this type of family, members are distant from each other, resulting in a great deal of coldness and emotional separation. They seem to care for each other, but their love is distant, undemonstrative, and often cold. A lot of personal separateness and independence exists. Here, individuals tend to be very autonomous and have many separate interests. There is either limited or rigid discipline where children are in control or constantly rebelling with attention-seeking behavior. Growing up, children need connection; in detached families this bond is severely inadequate, there is limited physical and emotional connection and here too, *children do not feel loved.*

A teenager told me, her parents would not tell her what time she should be home, causing her to be very confused. Since there was no parental structure, she made up her own curfew and she based it upon how much she liked the boy.

Enmeshed – Picture a bowl of spaghetti with no sauce. This is what an enmeshed family may look like from the outside, no real boundaries, like a bowl of noodles all intertwined, each person tangled beyond recognition. Knotted together family members do not know where they end and another begins. There is very little personal privacy with few outside friends or interests. Closeness in this family is to the extreme and no one can question family loyalty.

Discipline is a hodgepodge of permissiveness and explosive anger at real or imagined boundary crossings. Children are confused and uncertain for they know not where their parents' boundaries stop and theirs' begin. In this family, children learn to own other family member's emotions and problems, something not belonging to them. They discover how to manipulate and take advantage of this family system, and often wind up being in control of this family. Teenagers especially need a firm parental boundary to bump up against as they develop themselves different from the parents. When a teenager challenges this type of parent, they do not hit a hard structure, but a sponge.

The four distinct quadrants of the Circumplex Diagram are:
- **Rigidly - Enmeshed**
- **Chaotically - Enmeshed**
- **Rigidly -Disengaged**
- **Chaotically - Disengaged**

Some specific examples of how families balance their separateness versus togetherness in the *Cohesion* scale are:

> *On the Disengaged side*
>> little closeness
>> little loyalty
>> high degree of independence.

> *On the Enmeshed end*
>> high degree of closeness
>> high degree of closeness loyalty
>> high degree of dependency.

Flexibility is a measurement of the family's leadership, roles, and rules. Some specific examples are:

> *Highly Chaotic*
>> lack of leadership
>> dramatic shifts in roles
>> erratic discipline
>> too much change

> *Highly Rigid*
>> leadership dictator
>> strict discipline
>> roles seldom change

Comparing the balance between *Cohesion* and *Flexibility*, the further out toward the extremes on any of these continuums, a family may find themselves more out of balance, unhealthier, and unhappy. The closer to the center they are, the more balanced, healthy, and happy these families tend to be.

You might be a Chaos Person if...
you can resist anything, as long as
anything does not include temptation.

Communication

*"Every strike brings me closer
to the next home run."*
Babe Ruth

According to the Circumplex Model of Family Systems, communication is broken down into positive and negative directions.

Negative– Families find little room in negative communication for the sharing of feelings, goals, and daily activities. Talk around the supper table is limited with either little talking, or communication dominated by a select power group or individual. Roadblocks to effective communication are commonplace such as double-messages, criticism, double binds, lying, and denial.

Positive – Communication is a mutual experience where families share feelings, hopes, dreams, and goals. Problems are talked about with unconditional positive regard. Families do not let problems linger but rather work together to find healthy solutions.

When considering Flexibility and the Cohesion axis described by this model, as families learn to move toward the center positions and away from the four extremes, good communication leads the way toward desirable outcomes. As families learn how to listen with respect, acceptance, and understanding, they change these extreme patterns and more positive outcomes result.

I grew up in a family best described by the *Chaotic –Enmeshed* quadrant, not all the way out but maybe halfway between the extreme and the middle of the Circumplex Model. Much of our communication fell into the *Negative* dynamic. Although dysfunctional according to the model, we were very normal to our friends, relatives, and friends. In other words, most families find themselves to some degree in one of these quadrants. I know no family in the middle, the healthy area, unless they do considerable work toward achieving the serenity they seek. Remember: chaos might be what you know best but *peace is your birthright*.

Knowing the dynamics of the family you grew up in provides the understanding of where you came from. Although this knowledge begs the question, "Why did my family behave this way?" In exploring relationships, "why" questions seldom provide a helpful answer. Your challenge, which you accepted by reading this book, is deeper and more profound. The real question to ponder is, "What am I going to do with my history? Am I going to repeat my family dynamics and pass my dysfunction on to my kids or can I learn to live in the middle, in balance?"

Drs. David H. Olson, Douglas Sprenkle and Candyce Russell did not propose the Circumplex Model of Family Systems to blame families nor is it included to bash or shame families; it is for learning and understanding. There is much more to learn from the Circumplex Model than presented in this section. If you wish to continue what you learned, try the website www.facesiv.com.

Exercise 2

Healthy families live in the middle of this Family Extremes Diagram. This middle point is the healthy zone between any two dysfunctional extremes, a balance between being too enmeshed and too disengaged, and another balance between too rigid and too chaotic.

In the family you grew up in, did you find yourself in any of the extremes, if so, which one? Comparing your family with the Circumplex Model, what do you now notice about your family?

In the terms of the Circumplex Model, what quadrant best describes the family you now have today? Do you find your family in any of the extremes, if so, which one? How has this model helped change how you see your family?

Since you are now grown, your main influence is on the family you have now. Does your role in your family fall into one of the extreme positions? What can you do to help your family find a healthier balance?

Review the ***Positive-Negative*** communication effectiveness on a continuum, with positive on the right extreme and negative on the left. In the family you grew up in, how effective was your family communication? Did your family communicate positively, or was a lot of communication negative?

In the family you now have as an adult, how effective is your family communication?

What can you do to improve your family communication?

The Circumplex Model illustrates the various quadrants where families find themselves. Families with unmanaged stress and limited coping skills have an increased probability of winding up in one of the far ends of one of these quadrants. In the middle, families are neither enmeshed nor detached, neither chaotic nor rigid but maintaining a healthy balance. Families functioning in the middle are living in peace and not in the chaos so many of us sadly accept as normal.

Families do not intentionally desire extreme positions but tend to gravitate toward the extreme parts of these quadrants, especially when limited coping skills and poor communication compound daily stresses. This creates a spinning motion with the centrifugal effect of moving families toward the outer limits of this diagram.

You might be a Chaos Person if...
you are an egomaniac
with an inferiority complex.

If you desire to be in balance and currently are not, you now have a roadmap, a GPS to where you want to be. You have *no control* over your family history but *absolute control* over how you want to live your life now.

"It's the most unhappy people
who most fear change."
Migon McLaughlin

In *The Wizard of Oz,* Glenda the Good Witch told Dorothy, "Tap your heels together three times, and say 'There's no place like home.'" Following the Good Witch's instruction, Dorothy tapped her heels together three times, repeated the instructions, and then returned home.

Now I am the Good Witch with a magic wand, so repeat after me: "I am good enough...now."

Say it three times and, like Dorothy, you will begin your journey home – home to the giant, warm and comfortable room called *self-love,* a place where you once lived but for some reason left. When you were born, you came into this world full of self-love, joy, wonder, and awe. You were born with the bliss all babies have. Why would you not have this baby-like joy, since you just came fresh from your Creator!

Why anyone would ever leave this wonderful world of self-love is not the question. *Why* is often a very limiting question to ask about large life questions. The better question is, *How* are you going to get it back?...*How* are you going to go home?..."*How* am I going to go home?" is the real question.

Now, please say it again: "I am good enough... now. I am good enough...now." I am good enough...now." Hearing you say, "I am good enough...now" is music to my ears. Hearing you say this mantra, I am smiling, your Creator is smiling, and most importantly...you are smiling.

At one time in my life, I was like some people who think this exercise, *I am good enough,* is blowing smoke where the sun doesn't shine or a mess of psycho-babble. For me, as I look back on myself, I was so entrenched in my way of living that any change, even for good, was frightening. Although I was desperate, despising my life, the fear kept me paralyzed. I resisted change like Davy Crockett defended the Alamo against General Santa Anna. Even with Davy Crockett's best efforts, the Alamo fell and like Crockett, the pain of life won over my best resistance, forcing me to change. I had to surrender. I am so thankful for the pain convincing me to change. I hope you are smarter than me and maybe what you learn in this book can keep the pain at bay and still allow you to grow to peace and serenity.

Continuing with our Wizard of Oz theme, do you remember the song *Tin Man* by Dewy Bunnell? I love the refrain in this wonderful song: "Oz didn't give anything to the Tin Man that he didn't already have."

You are *good enough now* and if I were the Great and Powerful Wizard of Oz, I could not give you anything you do not *already have*. You are *good enough* right now. Humor me; let go of your natural resistance to allow sunshine into your darkness and say it again, "*I am good enough... now. I am good enough... now. I am good enough... now.*"

Great...can you hear the angels singing? I can. People often declare, in honest reflection, "*I do not know who I am.*" I celebrate their uncertainty. This self-confession is often necessary before the clarity of introspection can occur.

Remember, for people who live in chaos, this turmoil is normal. Resistance to allowing sunshine in is natural. Maybe not consciously but for chaos people this constant tension becomes their self-definition. If chaos is what is known and serenity is abnormal, confusion can occur when we find ourselves experiencing a wonderful state of temporary happiness. In this confusion, we lament, "I don't know who I am," for most do not remember ourselves in a peaceful state. A great deal of uncertainty and confusion will be your companion when struggling to escape the dysfunction morass. This model helps people discover who they really are, discovering and claiming the wonderful world of themselves. Will you allow this sunshine in?

"An unexamined life is not worth living."
Socrates

Giving up chaos is the price one must pay for the natural state of peace and serenity. Logically, we ask ourselves, "Why would anyone want to live in chaos?" Why would anyone want to live in darkness? Good question, but often we do and this is part of the struggle. Remember, if chaos is normal for a person, then a change to peace and serenity is abnormal and this change, however desirable, is difficult. After all, who would you be without your trusted state of chaos?

Are you ready for sunshine? Are you ready to change? As strange as these questions seem, especially since we just discussed the difference between chaos and peace, it is an important question. If the resistance to change is too great, nothing will happen; the status quo of chaos will trump peace and serenity. The necessary energy for change is required in order to have the drive necessary to sustain this change process. Without you putting forth the required force, this book will find itself on the shelf with all of the other unread self-help books collecting dust patiently awaiting your return.

Before I entered the mental health field, when I first moved to Baton Rouge, one of my vendors in the construction industry gave me a fifth of liquor for Christmas. I had been in recovery from alcoholism for some time and, at this point, I could use alcohol in a positive way...I could refrain from drinking. Since I was not about to drink this bottle and had no use for it, I gave it to my friend, Bob.

About six months after I gave the whiskey to Bob, he entered recovery. He was really getting a lot out of the AA meetings and discovering the wonderful world of Bob. When he had some recovery maturity, he posed a question to me. "David, before I went in recovery, did you know I was an alcoholic?"

"Yes, Bob, I really thought you might be."

"Then, my dear friend, why did you give me the fifth of liquor?" he asked.

"I thought you had not yet drunk enough, Bob."

What was I telling my friend? Like the balancing scale, Bob had not experienced enough pain associated with his drinking to break the bonds of change; he had not struggled enough. Once the scale tipped in the direction of change, when the pain of status quo was too excruciating, he clicked his heels together three times and said, "There's no place like home," and then began his journey homeward.

Change is scary. Change requires stepping out into the darkness of the unknown, leaving the comfort of the light, the known. This book shines light on the path ahead but the darkness will still shield part of this path. You will be the one who steps out beyond the light trusting there is solid ground beneath you.

Exercise 3

So again the question, "Are you ready to change? Are you ready? Do you want to go home?" If so, click your heels together three times and prepare to go home. Write about your answer.

You might be a Chaos Person if...
you have to dial long-distance
to get in touch with your emotions.

Part II – Family Sculpturing –

"Serenity isn't freedom from the storm...
it's the peace within the storm."
Shwana M.

Family members have certain patterns they tend to fall into unintentionally and these patterns are passed down from generation to generation. Sharon Wegscheider-Cruse uses a wonderful description of an alcoholic family that can serve as a model for understanding these dysfunctional family patterns.

Although she describes an alcoholic home, the behaviors are similar to most dysfunctional families. Even if your family did not include the disease of addiction, people often identify with this description to some degree. Regardless of your experience with addiction, explore this section looking for your own behavior patterns and see what you can relate to.

This section is based upon the work of Sharon Wegscheider-Cruse, from her book *Another Chance - Hope and Help for the Alcoholic Families*. Ms. Cruse generously granted permission to use her instructive model.

"The best time to plant a
tree was 20 years ago.
The second best time is now."
Chinese Proverb

Character Roles in Dysfunctional Families

Family members of dysfunctional families ignore their own needs in order to focus attention on the alcoholic. The designated abuser is the center of this type of family and family members unconsciously act out distinct "character" roles:

- Family Focus
- Chief Enabler
- Family Hero
- Family Rebel
- Mascot
- Lost Child

Even if your family was not addictive, see if you can identify with the description provided of the various roles. In this writing, I took the liberty of assigning these descriptions to one gender or another, not necessarily because one gender gravitates to one pattern or another, but because it makes the writing of these descriptions easier.

Family Focus

"Shame is the intensely painful feeling or experience that we are flawed and therefore unworthy of connection or belonging"
Dr. Brene Brown

Role in the family:
Focus of the family

To the outside world:
Blame, denial, hostility, charming, grandiosity, aggressive, self-pity, selfish

Inside feelings:
Guilt, anxiety, inadequacy, self-pity, shame, fear

This person is the centerpiece of the family and the entire family revolves around him and his addiction. He is often abusive, caustic, and threatening. Sometimes he is passive, aloof, and distant. In both extremes, he has a bubble around him preventing the love he may want to express; instead, his emotions often come out "sideways" in a hurtful, cruel, and controlling manner. There is a tongue-in-cheek joke Alcoholic Anonymous members sometime say: "Alcoholics do not have relationships...they take hostages." Although members chuckle when saying this, the humor lies in its basic truth.

Sometimes the active addiction does not happen right away but develops after marriage. However, this person already had these characteristics before he met his partner, but now since he has someone to be responsible for him, he is free to practice his addiction. Although we are using an alcoholic as our model, again the Family Focus can be addictive, compulsive, mentally ill, or anyone whose behavior fits this role.

Chief Enabler

*"If you do what you've always done,
you'll get what you've always gotten.*
Tony Robbins

Role in the family:
*Keep the family together, maintaining appropriate
appearances to others.*

To the outside world:
Saint, super-responsible, martyr, sarcastic, serious,
physically ill

Inside feelings:
Hurt, guilt, bitterness, fear, resentments, anger

The *Chief Enabler* (*Enabler*) is often the spouse, sometimes the parent, of the *Family Focus* (*Focus*). The *Enabler* over-functions in the relationship, while the *Focus* under-functions. As a result of the over-functioning, the *Family Focus* depends on the *Enabler* the most. Over time, this over-under functioning becomes more and more pronounced as the *Focus* loses control and the *Enabler* is increasingly more responsible to make up for the lack in her loved one. Percentage-wise, the *Enabler* is more often female than male. I am not sure why this pattern exists; perhaps it is the difference in raising boys and girls and/or each gender's natural tendency or maybe that women tend to adopt the nurturing role and men the hunting role.

The *Enabler* not only centers her attention on the *Focus,* but also tends to try to meet every family member's needs, losing her identity in the process. She protects the family by denying any problems with outside friends or relatives: "Nope, no problems in this family." Her denial is projected to the world. She attempts to keep everybody happy through placation and making excuses for unhealthy or dysfunctional behavior, while denying her underlying fears of inadequacy and helplessness.

Since the *Enabler* never takes the time to assess her own needs and feelings, she often comes across as emotionally aloof and superficial. Inside, she feels unfulfilled, disconnected, and out of control, as she becomes everyone else's caretaker. To the outside world, she looks like a saint but, inwardly, she dies a slow and painful death. Between the *Focus* and the *Enabler*...guess who dies more often from stress-related disease? Yep, you got it...the *Chief Enabler.*

Family Hero

*"If you don't like something
change it; if you can't change it,
change the way you think about it."*
Mary Engelbreit

Role in the family:
*Source of family pride/self-worth, maintains order
within the household*

To the outside world:
High achiever, dedicated, driven, "good kid," responsible, follows habits, caretaker, parental substitute

Inside feelings:
Guilt, loneliness, anger, fear of losing control, sensitive to

criticism, inadequate

The *Family Hero* is especially sensitive to the family's problems. The *Hero* usually is the oldest child, attached to the parents through emotions, and lives life according to the same values and behaviors as the parents.

Family Heroes are overly responsible for other family members' pain and as the *Hero* desperately tries to improve the situation...to fix it. In this role, often as the eldest, he functions as a surrogate parent and takes care of younger siblings, chores, and household responsibilities. He is compelled to achieve great success in some environment outside of the home to provide self-worth and, more importantly, the lacking positive recognition the family so desperately needs.

However, because this does not change the *Focus'* behavior, the *Hero* ultimately feels like a failure. The *Family Hero* tends to marry an unhealthy person, sometimes the next *Family Focus*, to start the cycle over again.

Family Rebel

"People often say motivation doesn't last.
Well, neither does bathing.
That's why we recommend it daily. "
Zig Ziglar

Role in the family:
> *Keeps focus off of parents*

To the outside world
> Hostile, defiant, "don't care" attitude, trouble maker, tough, cold, "cool", blames others, strong peer alliance

Inside feelings:
> Hurt, guilt, anger, rejection

The *Family Rebel* chooses to pull away from the family in a destructive manner, thereby bringing negative attention to herself by getting into trouble, getting hurt, or just simply withdrawing. Often the *Rebel* is the second oldest and feels rejected, receives mostly negative attention, often ending up chemically dependent, and is unable to express any true feelings. *Rebels* are at high risk for suicide, and they often project a wall between themselves and other people. Some describe *Rebels* as having "frozen tears", but to maintain their tough exterior they dare not cry, especially in front of others.

Since the family's attention is on this child, the family uses the *Rebel* as a scapegoat by focusing on her misdeeds and imperfections instead of admitting their part of the problem; it is part of the family's denial system. Spotlighting the *Rebel* gives family members a target to blame, allowing temporary escape from their own pain and isolation. *Rebels* tend to revolt but this acting-out behavior is really a cry for help whenever she feels consumed by feelings of shame, guilt, and emptiness. Having this spotlight on her and receiving the full lash of the criticism whip from her parents, this child feels a tremendous amount of rejection.

Often, the *Rebel* is the first family member brought into counseling, with the family expecting that if this child changes, everything will be okay. Ironically, it is often the *Rebel* who is the healthiest member of the family!

Mascot

"Every child is an artist.
The problem is how to remain
an artist once he grows up."
Pablo Picasso

Role in the family:
Comic relief

To the outside world:
Clowning, immature, cute, hyperactive, distracting, class-clown, life of the party

Inside feelings:
Anxiety, fear, insecurity

The *Mascot's* job is to draw attention to himself by providing humor, charm, and being the comic relief. He is the life of the party, becomes the class clown, and can light up the room with his effervescence. The party does not start until the *Mascot* arrives. He is responsible for family harmony by decreasing stressful situations and conflict with comedic distractions.

Under the mask of humor, fear and anxiety consumes the *Mascot*. This person often displays hyperactive behavior, can be a slow learner, a poor achiever, and tends to become very dependent on physical things

This type of humor becomes a diversion, temporarily decreasing tension; however, when the problems are not directly and honestly stated, his comic diversion actually prevents resolution. *Mascots* are terrified of rejection and struggle with intimate relationships by pushing others away with humor. They usually are not very good at handling conflict.

Lost Child

> *"Go confidently in the direction of your dreams.*
> *Live the life you have imagined."*
> Henry David Thoreau

Role in the family:
> *Relief, gives up personal needs, low demands, low maintenance*

To the outside world:
> Quiet, shy, solitary, few friends, avoids stress, avoids conflict, attaches to things

Inside feelings:
> Unimportant, anger, rejection, anxious, hurt

The *Lost Child*, usually the middle child, is the quiet-one. "This child causes us no problems" is the message often describing this child. *Lost Children* work very hard not to add to the already chaotic family so they avoid trouble, do what they are told, and melt into the woodwork.

Just like Harry Potter's invisibility cloak, they tend to disappear within the family.

The *Lost Child* is forgotten, ignored, and thinks she has to face her problems alone. This strategy results in loneliness and personal suffering. She attaches to things, not people, tends to be shy, and does not relate to others. She sits alone in front of the television or a computer, reads a book, or sits alone in her room. Due to the sedentary lifestyle and a lack of emotional fulfillment, the *Lost Child* tends to have issues with weight. The *Lost Child* avoids stressful situations, does not confront other's bad behavior, is a loner, and is usually more regularly sick. This child is very lonely, neglected, angry and guilty. She is invisible to the rest of the family and often marries an unhealthy person who resembles the *Family Focus* to continue the familiar family dysfunction.

Exercise 4

These roles are not divided up at the dinner table one evening: "Okay, who wants to be the *Rebel*? You? Okay, now who gets the *Lost Child*?" "I want that one." "No, I called it first." Children adopt them because these are natural defensive survival postures necessary in dysfunctional families. The more dysfunction exists, the more pronounced the roles.

Did you identify with one or more of the roles? Which one?

How about your siblings? What roles did they play?

The key question, if you adopted one of these roles growing up…is it working or not working for you today? Explain.

You might be a chaos person if...
you got kicked out of the airport for leaving
your emotional baggage unattended.

Exercise 4 - continued

As an adult, you no longer need a role for protection. Are you ready to dump your role and become real? What does being real mean to you?

Write about your role and that of your family members.

*"Better to light a candle than
to curse the darkness."*
Chinese Proverb

Exercise - 5

Draw a picture of your family members, complete with labels. Draw each person in a size representing the significance to you when you were a child, the more dominant the person was, the larger the size. Draw interactive lines between each person indicating what type of connection each had with the others. Were the lines between family members you experienced nurturing, stressful, tension filled, painful, missing, and/or toxic?

*"Don't wait,
the time will never
be just right."*
Napoleon Hill

You might be a Chaos Person if...
the drunk is loud, obnoxious,
makes a fool of himself,
then gets arrested,
and it is you who feels embarrassed.

Children Raising Parents

"The more you know who you are,
and what you want,
the less you let things upset you."
Stephanie Perkins

When a child is first born and a parent puts his or her little finger close to the newborn's hand, the child instinctively wraps its little finger around this outstretched pinky. This is an age-old pattern passed down from when humans first developed opposable thumbs; with this connection, the child and parent create a bond. When little hands hold parents' fingers, in that instant, the parents enter the child's classroom awaiting the lessons from this wonder of life they are now privileged to raise, name, and call their own.

No parent ever held a child up by the heels and declared, "I'm going to screw up this kid." However, parents often inflict unintentional wounds upon the child as their parenting skills are what they know best: patterns from their own childhood. Some methods are wonderful, while some do not work. Many are outright destructive. The best humans can hope for is the wisdom to learn from their experience, attempting to improve on their own childhood insights. With desire for improvement and by applying learning methods that work, we can reduce the same degree of dysfunction we learned and decrease the unhealthy patterns in our progeny.

No one I know had perfect parents, for if they were perfect, it would be child-abuse! Perfect parents would set a child up for what is unattainable in the real world of flawed people who love their children but have not yet found the wisdom necessary for flawless parenting.

Although love is a wonderful experience…*Love is not enough.* Love is the best humans have and it is certainly a desirable place to begin. What is missing is *how* to love, and eliminating these family roles and dysfunctional habits helps with this knowledge. Having children often provides an excellent reason for parents to learn better and more effective methods of expressing their love, unfortunately this learning often begins long after their poor coping skills have inflicted harm upon these little ones carrying their names.

As parents go, I was not a terrible parent. However, in reflection, I have deep regrets about how I raised my children, so I speak not as the all-knowing guru but as one who seeks forgiveness for my ignorance, abuse, and the dysfunction I inflicted upon my family. I seek absolution for using the only way of living I knew then. Now, I desperately seek new and better methods of loving. Today with this new learning, I could be a better parent; however, because of the ravages of time, I now do not have the necessary energy or the desire to raise children again. Maybe by passing on what I learned, you may not have to inflict the same pain onto your children, and my children's suffering will have meaning. *I certainly hope this is true.*

I am convinced God gives us children to teach parents. My children taught me my love wasn't enough and I needed a better way. My kids chuckle when I explain this wisdom knowing, yes, they "raised" their daddy. For if it were not for the pain I saw in their faces caused in large part from how they were raised, I would not have sought to find different solutions, thoughts, and better ways of relating to those I love. I am so thankful for the dysfunction in my family, for without the pain from those days, I would not have achieved the peace I so long sought. I hope now to shine a beacon from my lighthouse enabling my loved ones to navigate a course of sanity, and maybe when they see the positive changes in my life, it will give them permission to change and then to forgive me.

> *"Gratitude unlocks the fullness of life.*
> *it turns what we have into enough,*
> *chaos to order, confusion to clarity.*
> *It can turn a meal into a feast,*
> *a house into a home,*
> *a stranger into a friend."*
> Melody Beattie

You might be a Chaos Person if...
you act as your own prosecuting attorney, judge and jury –
and you are proud of your 100% conviction rate.

Part III - Dysfunctional Family Habits

In all families, there are certain dysfunctional habits passed down from generation to generation as family norms. When we interact with one another with destructive life patterns we wonder why *Love is Not Enough*. Parents did not invent these destructive habits, but each family member learns them, committing them to memory, ready to pass them on to the next generation. You will not see these dysfunctional family habits posted upon the refrigerator door, but rather these are learned at our parents' knees. You now have the opportunity to examine them in light of how you want to live. Shall you continue this pattern? Is there a better way of living?

My wife, Penny, tells a story about participating in parental dysfunction. One day, it was her turn to drive a car full of young children to school. Her two were in the front seat while in the back seat were four of the neighbor's kids. The back seat was full of normal squealing noise and childhood antics. In the front seat, her two engaged in their usual brother and sister squabbles, plus punching and poking each other. She endured it as long as humanly possible and in a fit of frustration with their fighting, she bopped both her kids. At the same instant, she yelled, "Stop that! I don't believe in violence!" Her sudden and emphatic declaration silenced all disturbances as the children realized they had exceeded this mother's endurance. She later told me she was thankful they were too young to see the irony of her behavior in contrast to her words.

Today, she makes us all laugh with this story, for we all remember our own fits of parental frustration, and we conjure up memories of receiving similar harsh reactions from our own parents. Her story conveys a deep truth. She did not intend to inflict this negative message or pain upon her kids, but it is easy to imagine the damage done in a fit of frustration. A "perfect parent" would not have reacted this way; since no one reading this book is perfect we can all understand the pressures on parents raising kids.

This is your chance to read these habits and explore their destructive force. Are these habits really what you want for your family and/or relationship?

Is there a better and more peaceful way of living? To grow, we must admit what does not work. More importantly, we must be willing to change. If you recognize that you too enforced these habits in your family, this does not make you a bad person. The fact that you are reading this book suggests you are willing to change and improve your and life skills. ***Congratulations.***

Many people grew up in homes having some unwritten habits everyone knew but never acknowledged, discussed, or chose. No one in these families had the right to protest, or even the inner wisdom to question their value, so they continued being passed on from one generation to the next, keeping generations of families in dysfunctional patterns.

Members of a dysfunctional family practice the habits they have been taught and expect within their family dynamics. Family members do not acknowledge these rules nor are they aware they exist; however, these habits are so entrenched into the family pattern they become iron-clad rules. Simply, families express these habits as *Don't* statements.

Don't Talk.

Don't Trust.

Don't Feel.

Don't Change.

Don't Be Real.

Don't Respect Boundaries.

Don't Accept.

When the *Habits of Dysfunctional Families* are in force,
happiness is often fleeting and severely limited.

Habit I - *Don't talk*

*...you will be more disappointed by the
things that you didn't do than
by the ones you did so..."*
Mark Twain

The first habit is *Don't Talk*. "We don't air our dirty laundry outside the family." Every family member knows this habit, embraces it, and follows its dictates. Learned chaos is habit forming! When mayhem is the norm, peace and serenity, which is the natural state, becomes so unsettling, family members play the Uproar Game to feel normal. And what is the "Uproar Game"? It is different for each family, but it is a pattern of behavior in which every family member participates and no matter the rules of the individual games, all players end with increased blame, anger, alienation, misunderstanding, and always hurt feelings.

Chaos limits the free-flow of love and becomes a roadblock to what family members want most and sadly, it becomes the normal for the family. Not talking about what is painful in the family is one of the habits created in dysfunction and permits the continuation of chaos, which allows everyone to continue to feel normal.

In my most dysfunctional days when I was raising my kids, one Sunday we were all going to church. While getting ready for church, we had a horrible fight, and everyone was mad at everyone else. It was total chaos, sad but normal for our family. We were all dressed in our Sunday's finest and when we pulled into the church parking lot and started to get out, my first wife, Sandi, made a profound statement, "Stop, don't get out yet."

We all waited for a moment in shocked silence as she said to the entire family, "We are going to get out of this car and I'm going to hold your arm and the kids will follow us up the sidewalk. We will smile at everyone, make small talk, and be pleasant. No one knows how painful it is living in this family."

With our rigid compliance of the *Don't Talk* habits, my family was not going to allow anyone to know about our dysfunction, our pain, because... "What would they think?" My wife's prophecy came true.

Since I was an elder in the Presbyterian Church, I had to look the part. I pulled my shoulders back; my wife grabbed my arm, as a "good" wife should. We smiled at everyone we met, shared polite pleasantries, and marched up those steps, keeping all the pain inside. Success, no one knew... *Don't Talk.*

Exercise - 6

If you grew up with the "no talk" habit, how does it affect your family today?

If this isn't the way you want to live your life from now on, what do you have to do differently?

You might be a Chaos Person if...
your anger management
counselor is the HULK.

Habit II – *Don't Trust*

People who are not in touch with themselves are not honest. I do not mean they are thieves or liars, but most have some external definition of themselves, a masterful degree of falseness. We wear masks hiding our true selves from others, thinking, "If you knew the real me, you would not like me. Since I do not like myself, how can anyone else really love me? Therefore, I can't let you in. I can't let you know me... for I am so ashamed."

As you read in the Family Sculpturing section, some of the roles family members tend to adopt are the *Hero, Mascot, Rebel, Lost Child*, and *Chief Enabler*. Some families shine a spotlight and focus on a dominant person, the designated victim, who is the center stage of this family. This person is often addictive, compulsive, mentally ill, or has just adopted this mantle of *Family Focus*. Family members not only have their own role-masks to hide behind, but they often develop their own special place to conceal their pain. Examples of places to hide are alcohol, drugs, perfectionism, gambling, rescuing others, extreme religion, overwork, obsessive success seeking, hoarding, obsessive compulsion, cutting/self-mutilation, eating disorders, excessive computer usage, game playing, telephone chatter... or it could be they are always talking or never talking, embracing the sadness of Pooh's Eyeore, or any one of countless other temporary escapes from pain.

While growing up, I adopted two roles. Since I was the only boy, I sometimes played the *Hero* role, trying to be perfect. Most of the time, my halo slipped and I degenerated into the *Rebel*. With the family I raised, I had two *Rebels*; both of my kids acted out the family pain by creating chaos (which was our normal) with unacceptable behavior such as drugs, sexual promiscuity, sneaking out, and trashing our family values (Remember, I was an elder in the Presbyterian Church and had to look the part.) I was very successful at hiding from other family members in alcohol, books, and disappearing into my workshop - anything to escape from connecting with the people I loved.

My first wife hid in perfectionism. She brutalized herself trying to live up to the unattainable definition of perfect. She placed these demands on the family and on her children. As great as this damage was, most of her destruction was self-inflicted. Even as unaware as I was back then, I knew she was in a great deal of pain.

Because of our untreated wounds, our expressions of love toward our children were often painful, lacking, not enough, misdirected, and with unintended consequences and collateral damages – a strange way of loving but it was the best my children received from their parents. We all wanted connection, intimacy, the warmth of a loving relationship, we wanted to hug and not tug but were afraid of its intensity. On the rare occasions when our family was peaceful, eventually one of the chosen antagonists created chaos-our normal-and then we all ran screaming back to the chaos we knew so well and had so well perfected.

Distrust is a byproduct when family members wear masks and hide. They are often physically present but are not there in spirit. *Don't trust* becomes normal and they live in isolation, wanting to feel close to others but not allowing the trust so necessary for happiness. Behind those walls, family members feel isolated, lonely, and not connected to each other. When not connected to ourselves, how can we connect to another?

People who do not trust metaphorically wear a protective covering behind which they hide. In the book *Iron Mask,* I wrote about seeing my daughter suffer behind her iron mask. I know how lonely this is for she copied my iron mask as she watched her father cope with his pain.

Family members who live in dysfunction do not trust each other or themselves. Penny, my second wife, overheard her stepdaughter talking to one of her friends. My daughter declared with great vigor and determination, "I'm going to read one book a day." The friend's wise counsel was, "You are setting yourself up for failure by making promises you can't keep. Read one chapter a day, otherwise you'll end up lying to yourself and then you become untrusting of yourself." Sadly, my daughter did not read one book a day or even one chapter. After many times of letting herself down, she probably does not trust herself.

Exercise - 7

This exercise is a place to get honest and look deeply within yourself. Think about trust. In what areas do you recognize that you are not available to others?

Is there an element of falseness about how you live? What are your secrets?

Can your family members come to you with any of their problems? Are you a good listener...do you listen or do you try to *fix-it* for another? Are you a safe place for others to bring their problems? Do they?

Describe where you hide and escape from being real?

Do you often tell lies when the truth would be easier? Do you have a habit of lying so others do not hear the truth? Write a little about it.

Do you embellish the truth attempting to make yourself look good to others? Are you living your life based upon what you perceive others may think? What does this cost you?

Are you an actor in your own life or merely a reactor to life? Explain.

You might be a Chaos Person if...
the reason you attend church is to increase
your capacity for being judgmental.

Habit III – *Don't Feel*

"We become what we think about."
Earl Nightingale

Feelings are not allowed to be expressed in this family except destructively. Since Mom and Dad do not know how to properly express their feelings, is it any wonder their children are also ignorant? Instead of acknowledging emotions and being honest about what is brewing deep within, dysfunctional families live in their thoughts, their minds; emotions are often too painful to acknowledge. Swirling in a squirrel cage of perpetual motion, the head-committee meets, argues, votes out the guidance available from emotions, successfully keeping serenity at bay and chaos close at hand.

When we took my son into drug treatment, one of the first things a counselor asked me was this: "Mad, sad, glad, fear, and hurt…which ones are good feelings and which ones are bad?" I looked at him with a blank expression. At that moment, I was completely emotionally numb. I did not know the difference between a feeling and a frying pan. My life was so painful then that I unknowingly shut down my emotions trying to protect myself. In this, I was successful – being numb did not hurt as much as if I allowed myself to experience the sharp edge of feelings. However, in shutting down, I also eliminated any possibility of glad and happy feelings. Even if they were something good, I could not feel the joy.

Being numb, I was emotionally void. In business meetings I was unable to look other people in the eye. This was unusual for me and it disturbed me greatly. How can you trust someone who will not look them in the eye? Now, I know what caused this numbness; it was a symptom of deep shame. I was feeling so miserable and self-loathing consumed me, crushing any possibility of joy. Life then was so painful; I could not stand the crushing weight of these feelings, so I looked for a shelter from the pain. Although I did not consciously make this decision, I became numb, and this numbness became my refuge, my place to hide.

Shortly after admitting my son in treatment, I started attending Al-Anon, the companion program for anyone who has a friend or relative with a drug or alcohol problem. (Does anyone *not* have a friend or relative with a drug or alcohol problem?) I was driving home from a Sunday night Al-Anon meeting in Kingwood, Texas thinking how my life had completely exploded: both my kids were doing drugs, my marriage had failed, and my business was on life support. It was a painful time, but the numbness kept me from feeling the incredible crushing weight of the shame, depression, and sorrow I experienced.

Surprisingly, as I drove away from the meeting, big old salty tears started to flow, clouding my vision, and I felt the pain. As painful as I was feeling, something else was occurring deep within me. Yes, I was in pain but I was also feeling...joy! "What a strange combination of emotions," I thought, "How can this be?" Then I discovered what was happening. Yes, I was in deep pain but I wasn't numb anymore. In the Al-Anon meeting, I broke the *No Talk* habit and shared about my pain and sorrow. I also broke the *No Trust* habit and trusted the members of the Kingwood Al-Anon Group. In breaking these family habits I knew and followed so well, I released all the emotions I had so carefully collected and stored. The dam of numbness so stoutly built had finally broken. I could feel. I broke the *Don't Feel* habit. I was again alive! From my self-inflicted numbness, I discovered incredible joy by becoming alive; I have not been numb since.

Exercise – 8

The Mood Chart (found on page 55) is a listing of the various human emotions available to help us navigate through life. They help us understand ourselves and communicate better with others. The primary words of the feeling language are Mad, Glad, Sad, Fear, and Hurt. Under each column are various other emotions in the same family as the five main words. Thoroughly read this chart and experience the full rainbow of the various feeling words available to express the many moods we may have.

There is a distinct difference in saying "I feel like..." and expressing actual emotions as listed on the Mood Chart. When using words in the Mood Chart you are actually identifying and expressing your feelings. There is a definite time to express your thoughts and a time to be honest about your emotions. Here is a challenge: For the next week, practice using the words on the Mood Chart to help others understand you, and for you to better understand yourself.

Mood Chart

MAD	GLAD	SAD	FEAR	HURT
Agitation	Admiration	Abandoned	Alarm	Aloof
Angry	Affection	Agonized	Anxious	Ashamed
Annoyed	Ardor	Bored	Apprehension	Belittled
Antagonism	Confident	Crushed	Bashful	Burdened
Arrogant	Cordiality	Deflated	Bewildered	Cheated
Bitter	Curiosity	Depressed	Cautious	Contempt
Contempt	Delight	Disconnected	Confused	Denied
Defiant	Desire	Disparaged	Distraction	Deserted
Disapproving	Devotion	Distant	Dread	Disappointed
Disdain	Ecstasy	Distraught	Embarrassed	Dismay
Disgust	Ecstatic	Distressed	Envious	Embarrassed
Enraged	Elation	Downcast	Evasive	Exhausted
Frustrated	Enthusiasm	Forlorn	Fearful	Guilty
Furious	Excitement	Gloomy	Fluster	Humiliated
Hostile	Fervor	Grieving	Frightened	Insulted
Indignant	Flush	Helpless	Horrified	Lonely
Irritated	Generosity	Hopeless	Hysterical	Mean
Livid	Happy	Ignored	Inadequate	Pain
Mischievous	Hope	Isolated	Insecure	Pained
Rage	Hopeful	Jealous	Menacing	Regret
Resentful	Inspiration	Melancholy	Overwhelmed	Shame
	Love-Struck	Miserable	Panic	Suffering
	Passion	Mournful	Pathos	Shocked

Do not discount the wonderful power of expressing yourself through the prism of the rainbow of emotions flowing through you. Want to be understood? Expressing emotion increases the potential of successful communication.

Please allow me to use a stereotypical male-female example to illustrate this point. Picture a stoic man. He has no expression on his face and it is difficult when looking at him to know what he is feeling. On the other end of the emotional-continuum is the overly emotional woman who acts out her feelings in a histrionic display. Both of these people are markedly disconnected from their feelings: the man hides behind the mask of stoicism and the woman hides in her histrionic antics.

The longest distance in the human experience is the 18 inches between the mind and the heart; sadly, most people's minds and hearts are disconnected. This disconnect causes the expression of love to often come out askew. The emotions go one way and the mind is racing in another direction. This causes your wonderful expression of care to come out perpendicular to the intent and inflict pain instead of the intended love.

Your emotions are your radar, allowing the user to navigate more successfully through life. When the radar is not used or if a person is unaware of this natural radar, then the result is like the Titanic: people without the benefit of radar run into the icebergs of life. The Mood Chart is your radar. By expressing yourself with this simple but wonderful tool, you can engage your radar and have it work for you. In this capacity, your emotions would be working for you, instead of against you.

Think of a conflict you had with a significant other. What would have happened if you had connected the emotions stirring inside you with the feelings you experiencing? These would be your honest feelings, right? Expressing deep, honest feelings seldom causes misunderstanding or hurt feelings. Telling the other person what you are feeling is honest and respectful.

Oh no, if you did that…you would be breaking three habits all at once: *Don't Talk, Don't Trust,* and *Don't Feel.*

Exercise - 9

On a scale from 1 to 5 with five being the most, how well are you connected to your emotions?

What do you think others' reactions will be if you use the Mood Chart to express what you are feeling?

Look at all these emotions. Go to the Mood Chart. What feelings come up for you when you think about getting honest and expressing your feelings to your loved ones? List them here.

You see two doors. #1 is "Stairway to Heaven".
#2 is "Committee to Study How to Get to Heaven".
You might be a Chaos Person if...
you pick door #2.

Now let's practice using this chart. Take the Mood Chart to your significant other and ask him/her to join you in this exercise. Give them the Mood Chart and ask them to express what they are feeling right now. After they express their feelings, repeat back to them what they said. "Okay, you said you are feeling annoyed, irritated, disappointed, and hopeful." By repeating their feelings back to them, several things happen. They will know you are trying to understand them. You will have a better understanding of your partner. They will hear their own emotions with your voice and have to own them. Do not try to judge your partner, explain yourself, change the subject, or discount what they tell you. No, your job in this exercise is to put your best listening hat upon your head and work towards understanding and acceptance.

Now, ask your partner to allow you to express your feelings and listen to you. This exchange of feeling words directly from the mood chart creates intimacy. Out of the billions of people on this earth this is the person you chose to be close to…profoundly close. This is what we desire in intimate relationships but this deep connection is often so frightful that most do not take advantage of the opportunities presented for honesty. Sharing the Mood Chart provides an artificial reason/a planned exercise/training wheels (pick your metaphor) for intimacy. Doing this exercise over a couple of weeks, you and your partner will enjoy an increased connection. All it takes is your willingness to do the exercise and get honest. Even if your partner does not want to share their deepest feelings, I encourage you to ask them if you can be honest with them. See what wonders can happen.

Keep a journal of the times you used this Mood Chart Exercise and record the results.

To challenge my daughter to break her dysfunctional habits, my wife, Penny told her, "All I want from you is to be real. No matter how ugly the truth, just be real." By asking her to get real with all emotions, not just the ones we would have liked to hear but also the unspoken ones causing the disconnection, Penny was inviting my daughter to break the *No Talk*, *No Feel*, and *Don't Trust* habits.

You might be a Chaos Person if...
you knew your boyfriend had a screw loose
and after you were married
you were determined to tightening it.

Habit IV – *Don't Change*

*"Because one believes in oneself,
one doesn't try to convince others.
Because one is content with oneself,
one doesn't need others' approval.
Because one accepts oneself,
the whole world accepts him or her."*
Lao Tzu

Change is threatening to the status quo. People growing up with these family habits embedded as norms become very uncomfortable with changing them. This is why people are often resistant about coming into counseling or to attending a self-help group such as Al Anon. In any change environment, and counseling certainly is one, there is a great fear of becoming introspective, expressing emotions, getting honest, and searching within for happiness. Even if you absolutely know getting honest is the beginning of a functional lifestyle, it is still very difficult to do.

Growing up, your parents probably did not teach you to be responsible for your own happiness and to rely on yourself for your joy. If you, like me, learned not to be responsible, then being responsible for your happiness becomes threatening to what you know – your normal. We learned it is someone else's fault for making us unhappy so we blame someone – anyone but ourselves – when troubled. In this blame game, we can hide and not be responsible.

"Mommy and Daddy are rigid, and this is the way families ought to operate." All family members know who they are supposed to be, their own position in the family pecking order, and their role in the family. So together we sing the Dysfunction Family Hymn... "This is the way we are, always shall be, Hallelujah, Hallelujah... Amen."

Even in dysfunctional families, most children experience some degree of love. However, when love is painful, children learn to equate pain and love. I think this was especially true when I raised my children. Both kids knew their daddy loved them, but my love sometimes came packaged with pain and shame and in this confusion, they learned to equate these two opposites together. When my kids looked for another to marry, they found someone like Momma and Daddy who loved them but inflicted pain. They sought the pain they knew so well and called it love.

Becky, a counseling colleague of mine told me about her neighbor Stacy banging on her door late one night. When Becky opened her door to allow Stacy to enter, she witnessed a woman bruised and bloody from her husband's beating. Becky welcomed Stacy in and washed her wounds then listened to Stacy's story of how her husband physically abused her. After hearing about this horrific experience, Becky said, "We need to report this to the police."

Stacy immediately declared, "No, no, now I know he loves me!"

This statement was so contradictory to what she expected; Becky gently asked her to explain. Stacy's explanation fit perfectly in the *Don't Change* habits, the toxic mixture of pain and love. Stacy explained how she grew up in a family where Daddy loves Mommy but Daddy also beats Mommy. This was her childhood experience, what she learned…love meant pain. Stacy continued to explain how she did not feel love from her husband when she was first married. He was so kind to her and she was not accustomed to anyone showing love with kindness. This kindness was not the love she had experienced and witnessed between her mother and father so she did not feel loved. She went on to explain how for the past few months she had been agitating him and creating many reasons for him to be angry with her. Now that he finally snapped and beat her, she said, "I now know he loves me!" This was her rationalization. This pain was what Stacy knew. It was her normal. Note: I am not excusing family violence as acceptable but this is an example of how entrenched a *Don't Change* Habit influenced this abused woman.

The professionals at battered women shelters often cite a statistic: it takes a woman an average of 13 times of leaving her spouse before she actually leaves him for good. People involved in battering relationships have all these family habits operating and *Don't Change* is one of the keys keeping them stuck in hurtful and violent relationships.

Think of a family as a child's mobile hanging from the ceiling. Each piece of the mobile is an individual family member and they are all connected together. Notice what happens when you move one family member: it affects the other family members. No family member exists in a vacuum or is isolated from the others. When you let go of the individual piece, what happens? Right, it returns to the original position. Many families have difficulty changing. They resist violating these family habits that are so deeply imbedded in their way of living. This is why one person changing in a family is so difficult. The family dynamics are rigid, set in stone; family members expect certain behavior from others. They know this pattern of behavior and therefore change – even good change – becomes threatening.

For ten years, I taught an anger management course for the Baton Rouge City Court. At the end of the sessions, I passed out a little card with my trademarked motto on it: *My Life Will Change… When I change!* ™ After one class ended, I went in the men's room and noticed this little card on top of the discarded paper towels. What a message this man sent to himself. Picture this, he was court ordered to anger management – obviously some part of his life was not working. He received a wonderful invitation to take personal inventory of himself and change. Instead of hearing this profound wisdom, he made a physical declaration to discard his power and threw away his choice to change!

"Holding anger is a poison.
It eats you from inside.
We think that hating is a
weapon that attacks the
person who harmed us.
But hatred is a curved blade.
And the harm we do,
we do to ourselves."
Mitch Albom

Exercise - 10

Did you receive *Don't Change* messages when growing up? What were they?

Who gave you these messages? How did you receive this message? What actions or words conveyed it to you?

In the past have you been unwilling to change? How has this resistance been working for you today? Has it kept you from the happiness you desire?

You might be a Chaos Person if...
you love your wife so much
...so much, you almost told her.

Habit V – Don't Be Real

Love is made up of three unconditional properties in equal measure:
acceptance, understanding, and appreciation.
Remove any one of the three and the triangle falls apart."
Vera Nazarian

Being real is hard for family members because they learned to adopt some form of protection to hide from others. Several examples of these protective masks are enabling, rescuing, being either over-responsible or under-responsible and/or wearing the victim badge.

If you plotted responsibility on a continuum where over-responsible is be on one side of the line and irresponsible is on the other end, dysfunctional families have both traits similar to the examples in the Circumplex Model. The more dysfunctional a family, the greater the extremes, it is easy to review this dynamic when using an extreme example like an alcoholic home. As his disease progresses, the alcoholic becomes increasingly more irresponsible and self-absorbed. As the dysfunction grows, the alcoholic's spouse assumes a greater and greater burden magnified by the alcoholic's lack of responsibility. They represent both ends of the *Over-Under* Responsibility Continuum. Family members can play the victim role at each end of the responsibility continuum as in, "Look what you made me do," or "If you loved me you would…"

In this example, why are the alcoholic and co-alcoholic attracted to one another? Why do they choose each other to fall in love with? Good question, but the hard truth is…they need each other. When they met, they found the perfect partner. The addictive person needs someone else other than him or herself to help the disease progress. The person attracted is also inflicted with the disease and needs someone to focus upon other than him or herself. The co-alcoholic focuses on the mate, instead of an actual addictive substance. This is a perfect match! The alcoholic focuses on alcohol and becomes increasingly irresponsible and the co-alcoholic has his or her own drug of choice, the alcoholic, and gravitates toward being increasingly over responsible.

Even homes not afflicted with addiction may also have one person assuming more responsibility and the other doing less. This imbalance causes resentments within the over-responsible and dependency with the irresponsible person and this dynamic becomes the destructive life-pattern not conducive to happy families. Although in this illustration we used an alcoholic family, this continuum certainly can be true in non-addictive families.

The last Christmas of my first marriage was especially sad. Everyone exhibited his or her own individual form of extreme acting-out behavior. I gravitated toward spending more time at work. When I was at home, I hid in my shop or read books. My ex-wife increased her compulsive drive to clean the house and decorate it perfectly, and the kids disappeared to various friends' houses. When time came for decorating the Christmas tree, my ex-wife was in her over-responsible, high gear of perfectionism. From past painful experiences of her perfectionism, no one wanted to help Mom decorate. No one could meet her high standards, so instead of a family fun experience, she decorated it alone. As her perfectionism increased, the rest of the family reacted by not being there physically. We missed the happy family opportunity of enjoying this tradition. Sad.

Our behavior became our defense mechanism. Being real was too scary, so we hid behind our walls of isolation. The tree that year was perfect, showroom beautiful, but with no personality. Since none of us participated in decorating this tree, nobody had any ownership; this beautiful tree was not ours. Sadly, the tree represented our family pain: beautiful on the outside but cold and dead on the inside.

Exercise - 11

With whom do you *over* function in your relationships? In what areas do you take responsibility for others when it really is not yours to take?

Are there areas where you *under* function and you do not take the responsibility you need to?

How successful are you in taking this responsibility for *YOUR* happiness? Where do you fall short?

What areas do you see yourself not being real, not being honest?

After cementing these dysfunctional habits in place, family members often see themselves as victims. A victim evokes sympathy, right? Victims are not responsible, right? Victims have the moral high ground... someone else is causing the misery, right? Victims can easily justify why they are right. Victims allow themselves to be stuck in the status quo and they excel at seeing the faults in others, ignoring their own responsibility. They love to take others' inventory of faults and are excellent at blaming. Victims become hypersensitive to real and perceived injustice, where any slight becomes a reason to reject. Victimization is the toxic wind blowing through families, fanning the fires of dysfunction.

When wounded by others, I often went hid in quiet places to lick my wounds. I could talk myself into being a self-righteous victim, expounding upon all the wrongs others did to me. As I was writing this exact section, my wife confronted me about not helping her with the yard. She did not belittle or attack or attempt to humiliate me, but compounding the sting, I knew she was right. I retreated to my quiet place and thought how hurt I was. I wallowed in my misery and self-righteousness for a moment; this was my tendency to hide in being a victim. Once I acknowledged my victim tendency, I then understood how I hurt the woman I love… a stark contrast to my first marriage, thinking how I blamed her, thought how unfair she was, and planned my defense. Once I got my center back, I knew I owed Penny an apology, and shortly thereafter made my amends -- victim *no more*. Hey, didn't I just break a family rule by violating this habit?

Exercise – 12

Write about areas where you see yourself as a victim.

How do you act when choosing the victim mode?

How is this posture of under/over functioning or being a victim working for you?

Does this attitude work toward a solution or compound the problem?

How does your over/under functioning increase or decrease the flow of love?

You just got out of a bad relationship
best described as a roller coaster.
You might be a Chaos Person if...
you immediate buy another ticket
on the next ride.

The opposite of victimization is the wonderful little sentence that so impressed me I trademarked it. I wanted it to be the overriding principle not only of my practice but my life. I encourage you to adopt this potent insight; this message is the *minimum* I want you to learn from reading this book:

My Life Will Change… When I Change! ™

In my first years in practice, I had this slogan printed on a sheet of paper, which I gave to each client. Now, I give them a green refrigerator magnet card carrying this profound message. One client was doing a line of cocaine on a sheet of paper, the same paper where I printed this message I had given him at our last session. After he snorted it, he looked down at this paper and read, "*My Life Will Change…When I Change.*" He told me, "Reading this message pissed me off so badly, I jumped in the car and came straight here to see you." I think I ruined his high!

Several years ago, when I was an adjunct professor at University of Phoenix, a student was telling the class about a job she'd landed a few years ago. On her first day in her new office, she noticed a green magnet card on one of the filing cabinets. She went over to it and read: "*MY Life Will Change… When I Change!* ™" Over the next three years in that job, every day she'd glance at this little green magnet with these inspiring words.

She then turned to me and asked, "Do you give out green magnets with that slogan on them? I nodded. "Yes, what you saw was probably *my* logo magnet."

"You're kidding!" she exclaimed. "After staring at this message for three years that's what made me decide to go get my degree. I can't believe it was your sticker!?!" She looked at me in disbelief of the coincidence, "…and you are my first professor!"

As simple as, "*MY Life Will Change… When I Change!* ™" is, most people have yet to incorporate it into their lives. However, once this becomes your guiding principle, you become a warrior for happiness and contentment. Look at this motto as your weapon to keep victimhood at bay protecting your hard-earned serenity.

Exercise – 13

What would happen if instead of you pointing your finger at others, wanting them to change so you could be okay, you pointed your two thumbs back at yourself and declared, *"My Life Will Change... When I Change!"*™ *Pointing* thumbs at ourselves and following this profound wisdom is *Thumb Work*.

What would happen in your relationships if you would spend more time pointing your thumbs at yourself instead of pointing your finger at others? How hard would this be for you?

Finger Work is the opposite. When we focus on other people by pointing our fingers at them, it is easy to list their faults and take their inventory. Once this inventory is compiled, it is easy to send them an emotional invoice demanding payment of any past transgressions, real, perceived, or imaginary. In the state of finger pointing, you may say words like "...to me," or "...on me," and list all you have done "for them." You may even use the manipulative approach and say, "If you loved me..."

List examples of when you did *Finger Work* with your significant other.

What does your partner see when you are pointing your finger at him/her?

Before you make this decision of fingers vs. thumbs, ask yourself this profound question: "What will it cost me to give up my righteous state of being the victim, point my thumbs at myself, and focus on the only part of the equation I can change…me?" What would happen if you did not point your finger at others and spent more time pointing your thumbs at yourself? What would this change cost you?

What do you think gets the best results…*Finger Work* or *Thumb Work?* It is your choice. Are you going to be irresponsible and point your finger at another, or be responsible and point both your thumbs at yourself searching for your part of the problem?

You might be a Chaos Person if…
you're so overcommitted,
you had to hire a stand-in
for your own funeral

Habit VI – Don't Respect Boundaries

> *"I am my own biggest critic. Before anyone else has criticized me, I have already criticized myself. But for the rest of my life, I am going to be with me and I don't want to spend my life with someone who is always critical. So I am going to stop being my own critic. It's high time that I accept all the great things about me."*
> C. JoyBell

Families living in dysfunction seldom have healthy boundaries. Dysfunctional families have trouble knowing where they stop and others begin. A vivid example is the alcoholic dad who took all the doors off the hinges to everyone's room but his. None of the family members had a place to all their own.

Here are several examples of simple boundary violations: using a sibling's toys without permission, looking in Mother's purse and finding coins for ice cream, or using Daddy's tools without permission or disrespectfully talking back to parents. Parents disrespect their children by yelling at their kids or not listening to them.

These are real boundary violations and all exhibit a lack of respect. When not respecting boundaries becomes the family norm, family members learn to violate others and create an environment where boundaries have fuzzy gray areas that are easy to cross. The reaction to this lack of respect is either by passively melting under the power of authority or the opposite – reacting violently when others do not show the proper respect.

A great way to study healthy and unhealthy boundaries is to watch *Supernanny, Nanny 911,* or other childcare shows on TV. These programs are an excellent way of learning how to have healthy families. Just observe the lessons Supernanny presents and listen to her wise counsel. During one show, a mother repeatedly kept physically grabbing her children. Supernanny quietly told her not to but she persisted. This grabbing showed lack of respect to the child. To illustrate what Supernanny was trying to tell this distraught mother, she started grabbing the mother. Finally, the mother yelled, "Stop it!"

Supernanny responded, "Exactly."

You could see the wisdom enter the mother's eyes, as she understood the violation she committed upon her children. Supernanny teaches how to put discipline in families where it was sorely lacking, but most importantly, she also teaches how to do it with *respect*.

Exercise - 14

Watch several episodes of *Supernanny* or *Nanny 911*. Even if your children are teenagers or have left home or even if you live alone, what you learn from these actual live families will help you have a better understanding of healthy boundaries. Return to this page and write about what you learned from *Supernanny* or *Nanny 911*.

You might be a Chaos Person if...
you are so wishy-washy you make
Charlie Brown look decisive.

While I was growing up, when in conflict with my dad, my sister would become upset, storm out of the room, and lock the door to her bedroom. My dad followed her upstairs and demanded that she unlock her door. Dad thought locking doors on him was disrespectful; plus he could not stand to see his family members unhappy. He assumed it was his job to fix everyone's pain. One time, when she refused to open the door, he broke through it. This was Dad's way of "showing love". My dad, like many of us, lived in his head and did not allow his emotions to guide him. Instead he ignored his emotions thus allowing them to unwillingly control him.

When my Dad had these strong emotions but was not connected with what they were telling him, he became intoxicated with his feelings; he was *emotionally drunk*. When emotionally drunk, the love he felt and tried to express often did not produce the results he intended and his feelings came out sideways in overreacting resulting in what he really did not want…disrespect.

The only way he knew to love was to be responsible for others happiness and when they were not, he took it as his job to fix it. He became overly responsible; which manifested as assuming responsibility for others' happiness. In his mind, breaking down the door was the way to solve the problem and ultimately make everyone happy. Breaking down the door removed the barrier to fixing the unhappy person; however, what he did was make a bad situation worse. These thoughts and behaviors were not because Dad was some kind of a monster; quite the contrary, they were actually done out of love. However, it is very hard to show love when *emotionally drunk*. This behavior backfired on Dad, his love was not working, and my sister, although she knew her father loved her, did not feel the love he was attempting to give.

When my own kids stormed into their rooms, like my father before me, I broke down their doors. I had adopted my father's attitude: someone's unhappiness was mine to fix. I also wanted my family members to be happy, so in my most dysfunctional thinking, breaking down the doors would fix their unhappiness. It is easy to see the insanity of this thinking but when *emotionally drunk*, my rational brain was not fully engaged, and others paid the price for this lack of connection.

Dad and I both had a boundary problem. Did my dad cause me to violate my children's boundaries when I, like my dad, broke down doors? No, although this was a learned behavior and I grew up thinking this is what a dad does. However, in truth, I was responsible for violating my loved one's boundary, not my father. I deeply regret my behavior.

> *"Discipline yourself before*
> *you discipline your children."*
> Ross McElwee

Boundaries represent awareness, knowing what the limits are and then respecting those limits. I now know where another person stops and I begin. With my new coping skills, faced with a similar situation and my daughter behind a locked door, I would quietly knock and ask her if she wanted to talk. If she did not, I would let her have her space and quietly tell her that when she did, I would be available... this is respect.

In therapy, I encourage couples having marital difficulties to each think, "What is the bottom-line behavior I expect from my partner?" Until each person knows about their deal-busting boundaries, how can they draw the line in the sand with their partner? Once they delineate the minimum behavior, the second step is to articulate these boundaries as their minimums to their partner. If people do not know their own boundaries, how can they defend a boundary they are not sure exists? How can another know where these boundaries are unless there is clear communication?

After the couple discusses their bottom-line behavior, I then encourage the couple to define the dream, "What do you want your relationship to be?" Once defining the minimum, the dream is then possible. Until you set the boundaries, you do not know what is on the other side. If no one has boundaries...how can there be any transgression? A word of caution: Do not make an absolute boundary you are not prepared to defend, and to follow through with the declared consequence.

Boundary violations are deeply experienced. Usually, a person who experiences a lack of respect feels violated. If that person never learned healthy boundaries when growing up, they could then react violently to perceived injustice. "Look at what you did to me" is the common refrain and then with a victim's posture, justifying a strong and often unhealthy response – *Finger Work.*

My first wife and I experienced an ongoing and escalating tension in our marriage. Especially in social settings, we would joke with one another. This humor was hurting, angry statements couched in terms of a joke. If the other responded in irritation, the common retort was "I was only joking" or "What's the matter with you? Can't you take a joke?!" These "jokes" were angry verbal barbs tipped in the poison we felt toward one another. Since we did not know how to deal directly, we attacked in the form of destructive humor. We violated each other's boundaries with verbal missiles of anger disguised in the pretense of "just kidding."

Exercise - 15

What boundary violations did you experience growing up? Which ones still exist today?

Are your boundaries pretty well defined now? How do they need improvement? Have you expressed your boundaries to your significant other? "

"And where there is no law
there is no transgression;"
Romans 4:15

How can you articulate them in a healthy way and then defend your boundaries? What do you need to change?

You might be a Chaos Person if...
your dignity always
dissolves in alcohol.

Habit VII – Don't Accept

*"You learned to accept, or you ended up in a small
room writing letters home with Crayolas."*
Stephen King

Dysfunctional family members become experts on focusing on others
and developing a keen ability to take other people's moral inventories.
After finding them lacking, the dysfunctional family member has justi-
fiable reasons for rejection…*Finger Work.* Having a finger pointed at
someone else provides a secure place where fear keeps introspection at
bay.

It is very difficult to develop a proper sense of self-esteem in a dysfunctional family. Having very little self-worth, looking at one's own character defects becomes so overwhelming there is no room for inward
focus. People so afflicted think: "I need to keep you from knowing me.
I have already rejected me, but if you knew how flawed I am, you
would also reject me…and since this is all I have, I could not stand any
more rejection. I am not worthy of someone understanding me so you
will not get the chance...so I must judge, reject, attack, and/or find fault
with you. I don't accept me so how can I accept you?"

They hide this low self-worth with exaggerated self-defense mecha-
nisms. Some bury themselves in not allowing others to notice them, as
the *Lost Child;* or they hide in exaggerated arrogance:"I am okay but
you definitely are not." Both extremes are defenses built around low
self-esteem. People build defenses around a weakness, not around
strength. Where self-esteem is strong, a defense is unnecessary.

When this low self-worth is hidden, one can understand why the person
becomes hypersensitive to the opinions of others and has a great deal of
difficulty accepting criticism no matter how warranted or gently said. If
confronted or criticized, the normal reaction is to take cover, run from
the truth, or attack back with the intensity of a Spanish Inquisition per-
secutor. Being judgmental is a form of attack keeping others off balance. Many are reluctant to face and deal directly with people who have
this type of controlling behavior.

Growing up in this type of family destroys the natural innocence individuals have at birth. These wounded children become all-knowing, have all the answers, and develop rigid beliefs. They gravitate to religions requiring conformance to absolutes, join political groups where their point of view is always correct, or participate in other groups that demand absolute conformance. In this atmosphere they sharpen their lack of sensitivity to other's opinions. Compromise is difficult for them. *My way or the highway* becomes their motto; *You are either for me or against me,* as they retreat into self-limiting black or white thinking. Since children from dysfunctional families are so good at judging others, they also judge themselves unacceptable when compared to others, always assuming they are second best, never enough. This is a painful realization, often hidden behind righteous arrogance.

When in this judgmental mindset, where they are right and you are wrong, they are quick to censure. Blame allows a safe place without requiring responsibility. I moved to Baton Rouge in 1989 and rented a townhouse. When I could not find something around the house, my immediate reaction was to look for someone to blame...and *I was living by myself!* There was no other person, yet this was my mindset: find someone to blame! However, by this time, I had gained some self-esteem and was now doing *Thumb Work* instead of my usual judgmental *Finger Work.* And hard as it was, I was able to point thumbs at the correct person...me.

Children who learned this set of dysfunctional family habits have difficulty letting their hair down and having fun. They lack the spontaneity of letting their little inner child play, allowing their perception of what others may think to control their own happiness and joy.

When I was studying substance abuse counseling, our professor at the University of Houston told us how difficult it was for her to have fun. Since she was now doing *Thumb Work* on herself and wanted to let go of her rigidity, her solution was to put child-like fun in her life and the only way she knew how to do this was to schedule it! So on Friday evenings she would *schedule some planned spontaneity!* Can't you picture reading this professor's day timer, "Friday, May 7, from 6:30-10:00 PM - *SPONTANEITY*."

> **You might be a chaos person if...**
> when you finally get in touch with your
> inner child you started wetting the bed.

Exercise - 16

How would you rate your self-esteem? If you recognize that it is low, what is it like living with your low self-worth?

Do you want to be around a person who is constantly criticizing you? Probably not, but if you are your main critic…do you want to be around you? What areas are you most critical of yourself?

What would it be like to have a healthy self–esteem?

When are you most likely to you point your finger of blame at another and criticize?

Who receives most of your criticism? What do they think about you?

Do others label you judgmental? If so, how does this affect your relationships with them?

If you harshly judge yourself, what does this condemnation do to your self-esteem?

Do you have difficulty having fun? What would it be like to live spontaneously, enjoying life and being free from what other people may think?

Can you play and be okay? In what areas are you willing to let go and have fun?

You might be a Chaos Person if...
you are so fearful of commitment
you turned down the opportunity
to join Jehovah's *Bystanders.*

Opposite of Acceptance

"Some wounds are permanent;
you know that as well as I do.
And the worst ones are invisible."
Blake Northcott

What is the opposite of acceptance? Most people think of these words: refusal, rejection, and disapproval – maybe it's being turned down, rejected, or denied. All of those are true, but in the context of dysfunctional habits, the opposite is control. Controlling others is the cornerstone of dysfunctional families.

The more dysfunctional, the more some family members seek to control the behavior of others. The controlling person is often a person in a position of authority such as a mother, father, or even a child. In this capacity, they attempt to manage the outcome of something they have little or no control over. The controller wastes energy by focusing on that which he/she has no control.

Since the controller does not talk directly or honestly about what is bothering him, except by hollering, baring his teeth, and freaking out about what is not being done to meet his specifications, his frustration grows. Often these expectations are in the form of perfectionism, an image created in the image in his mind of perfection and family members must perform according to this preconceived picture of perfection. Family members living with this demand learn survival techniques to coexist with this angry person who constantly demands perfection. Under this aura of perfection he knows how flawed he really is but his intact denial system keeps this awareness suppressed in the far recesses of his mind.

Using the Trait Continuum, we know life is a series of extremes on a scale. The Quality Continuum has perfection on one end and apathy on the other. The controlling perfectionist has gravitated toward one end of the continuum and is living out of balance. They are not bad people because of their desire to do things correctly but this strength becomes harmful when it gravitates out of balance toward one end or the other for it often results in controlling others.

My first wife was a perfectionist and took many opportunities to point out my obvious imperfections, which, I might add, held fertile grounds for improvement. In her rush to keep the house perfect, she sometimes asked me to make the bed. Since I already knew I was going to be criticized and I did not have the self-esteem to be honest or set boundaries, or even assertively stand up for myself, I acted out my frustration and did a half-assed job. She of course criticized me, but my saving grace of not doing my best allowed me to protect my tender and very limited self-esteem from the full impact of her criticism.

Controlling, demanding statements come with underlying messages that are harmful to those receiving them. What the person receiving these control messages hears from the controlling person is: "You are weak; I am strong. You cannot be successful without me. You cannot leave me. Without me, you could not survive."

> *"... it far easier to forgive others for being wrong than being right."*
> J. K. Rowling

Exercise - 17

What are your own controlling tendencies?

Are you living with perfection (yours and/or another's)? How do you act out your frustration? Is it working for you? Does it increase or decrease the flow of love?

How would your being honest help in both these examples? How would your life be different?

You might be a Chaos Person if...
the only way you can have a good day
is for someone else to have a bad one.

These habits of dysfunctional families are the norms families unknowingly adopt, maintain, and live by. Although they may seem to be set in stone, I know from breaking my own pattern, *change is possible*.

Exercise – 18

Now that you are an adult with your own family (I am assuming), are there any dysfunctional habits in place affecting your family today? What are they and what chaos are they creating?

You might be a Chaos Person if...
you and your boyfriend could
not communicate, so you got married.

A parent talking to his adult child explained, "If I caused 90% of your problems you have today because of how you grew up…then as a grown-up, you are responsible for 100% of how they affect you today."

Word of Caution

Even if you change for the good and other family members appear to appreciate the metamorphosis and applaud your transformation, they may secretly resent it or be frightened by this change. Dysfunctional families are rigid and if one member breaks the *No Change* habit and crushes established family norms, this change becomes a threat to the family dynamics, the status quo. When someone obtains peace and serenity, this shines a bright spotlight on others' own unhappiness making their discomfort even more apparent. They often react by attacking the changed person, belittling the change, trying to subvert progress, or by running away. The other and more desirable possibility is they are attracted to the change and see a pathway to begin their own journey. Here your changing becomes the lighthouse for their navigation. Just as one part of the mobile affects the entire system, if one person changes, it affects all those tied to the same family. This change is uncomfortable so the physics of the mobile and the tendency of the family is to return to status quo.

When a person changes, other family members do not know how to deal with the new person. They actually may like the changes, but it is such a contrast between what they knew and what they now experience that they may not know how to relate to the new person. They wait for the other shoe to drop: "When is Dad going to return to being the *Daddy-Jerk* they remember so well?"

When I started changing my life from mayhem to peace, it happened rapidly. Within six weeks instead of restless, irritable, and discontented, I became happy, joyous and free.

After doing considerable *Thumb Work*, my joy of life returned. Then I experienced a strange reaction from my teenage daughter; when I wanted to spend time with her, she did not want anything to do with me. If I got to see her, she had to know when I was going to pick her up and when I was taking her home; an hour and a half was the most she would commit to seeing her old man.

After eight months of this rigid limitation, she came to live with me. She then asked me a profound question: "Do you want to know why I did not want to have anything to do with you for the last eight months?"

"Yes," I said emphatically, surprised she knew how long her isolation had been. And I was shocked by her response: "Daddy, I saw you change and I did not know who you were."

She knew the Daddy-Jerk but the Daddy who was calm and peaceful; the Daddy who listened to her and did not try to control her was alien to the chaos to which she had become so accustomed. I was now breaking all the family habits she knew so well. I am sure she liked the change but she did not trust the change; she was waiting for me to return to what she knew best...*Daddy-Jerk*.

In arguments with my then estranged wife, she would throw out the chaos bait I knew so well and before I changed due to my *Thumb Work*, I would always bite and we would engage in the hurtful conflict to which we were so accustomed. One time, I did not fight back but said, "I am choosing not to react to that." Since this was not my normal reaction and I did not bite the bait as she anticipated, she immediately fired back, "Don't use that psycho-babble BS on me!"

At this moment, I had a choice: I could bite the bait for it looked so inviting, and participate in the chaos I knew so well, or I could not bite the bait. My response was uncharacteristically calm when I said, "You know, you and I fought for twenty years and I don't want to do that anymore."

She thought for a moment and said, "You know, you are right. I don't want to fight any more either." Here we were both breaking the *No Change Habit*! After this agreement, we had a respectful conversation.

When you change from chaos to peace, others may like the change but, like my daughter, may not trust the change. That is okay; you are changing for you, not for the approval of others. Ultimately, if the changes create a more peaceful lifestyle, they will be attracted to your new happiness. Calmness, joy, and contentment are attractive qualities. Your positive change sends out ripples on your family pond; these ripples will grow into tsunamis of positive energy affecting many people in this generation and many generations to come.

Note: As a Licensed Professional Counselor (LPC) I am required to provide a *Declaration of Practices and Procedures* to the mental health clients I see in treatment. Below is a portion of this document warning about the change process. It is included in this book for I also want you to know about the dynamics and potential results of change.

During the counseling experience other issues may be uncovered which at the beginning of the counseling relationship you did not anticipate. Successful counseling involves change and this growth is the opportunity the counseling environment provides. Change in relationship patterns resulting from therapy may produce unpredicted and/or possible adverse responses from other people in your life.

In the realm of significant relationships, some marriages/relationships will grow from the counseling experience and become stronger (this involves change on both partners). However, other people in the relationship may choose not to change. Studies have shown that when one person in a relationship changes and the other does not or changes in a different direction, this can lead to the dissolution of the marriage/relationship (especially very rigid ones).

Always remember to take yourself out of physical danger.

Exercise - 19

What do you suppose will happen to those you love if you change?

How will they react differently to you if you change for the better?

You might be a Chaos Person if...
the image you created finally came apart
when the Wizard of Oz
wanted his curtain back.

By-Product of Change

The Family Roles and the Habits of Dysfunctional Families create a set of maladaptive behaviors called *codependency*. Picture Mom and Dad covered in mud. If you lived in the same house with them and they dropped mud everywhere they went, how long would it take before you too were muddy?

Everyone reacts somewhat differently to traumatic experiences. In my role as a Critical Incident Crisis professional (CISD), I am called into organizations when a robbery, murder, suicide, explosion, or some other destructive experience has occurred. I conduct a debriefing session, sometimes in a group and sometimes individually. In this capacity, I assist the participants with their start to return to their normal selves before the incident. When people share their experiences, they begin to normalize what has happened, thus reducing the shock impact of the event. This lifting of the emotional burden changes the negative impact and goes a long way in preventing posttraumatic stress problems. These horrific events have taught me that not every employee has the same reaction to the same event.

Everyone reacts somewhat differently to traumatic experiences. In my role as a Critical Incident Stress Debriefing (CISD) specialist, organizations call me when a robbery, murder, suicide, explosion, or some other destructive experience has occurred. Here, I conduct a debriefing session with those impacted, in groups and/or sometimes individually. Here, I assist the employees with their journey back to normalcy. When people share their experiences, they begin to get their arms around the event and normalize what has happened, thus reducing the shock impact. This lifting of the emotional burden changes the negative impact and goes a long way in preventing post-traumatic stress problems. Interacting with employees after one of horrific events has taught me that not every employee has the same reaction to the same event.

Not every family member reacts the same to how they were raised; different family members often have their own unique set of behaviors. Some go on to lead successful and happy lives, while most others adopt many behaviors limiting the possibility of a happy and love-filled life. This set of harmful coping skills is also referred to as codependency. The Chaos Habits we just discussed are included in this set of destructive ways of thinking and reacting to life.

This next section includes an essay by Joanne T. entitled "*The Truth Is.*" Because she only uses the initial of her last name and maintains her anonymity, I assume Joanne is involved with a Twelve Step program. I received it from one of my fellow 12 Steps friends in Kingwood, Texas. If I had to guess which program she was involved in it would be Adult-Children of Alcoholics (ACoA). I wish I could meet her someday and thank her for the inspiration her essay has given to me and many others. I used this without her permission for without her last name it was impossible to give her full credit; maybe someday she will come out of her self-imposed anonymity and I will gladly credit her for writing this wonderful and powerful essay.

You will discover that how you were raised is a key factor in your degree of codependency. Often people want to know *why* they are so unhappy, miserable, and disconnected. People often are stuck on the question *"Why?"* Focusing on "why" often results in self-abuse and being stuck in the problem. A better question is, "Okay, you described me…now what am I going to do about it?" A better query is to ask yourself, "Do I want a happy life, or shall I continue in the same old destructive patterns my family has been doing for thousands of years?"

I divided Joanne T.'s essay into three parts. The first part concerns the problem. The next section is about healing, and the last part focuses on forgiveness. Her writing is italicized and my comments are regular text. Here is part one.

Part IV - The truth is...

Problem

Our parents did the best they could; they did not intend to hurt us. They had injuries from their past that kept them from being able to be there for us emotionally, to parent us in the way a little child needs ... they abused, neglected, and/or abandoned us: physically, emotionally, and/or spiritually. This childhood wound causes codependency.

Parents (or our major caregivers), who are hurt themselves and are hiding their own feelings and pain from themselves, are not real and present to themselves; therefore, they cannot be present and available for their children. Most often, they have some form of addictive or compulsive behavior to cover their own pain. This causes them to abuse, neglect, or abandon us in thousands of different and sometimes subtle ways.

We, as little ones, could not see our parents (our Gods) as bad; therefore, we decided that we were bad. Children do not have a frame of reference to judge parents and by taking responsibility for their parents, they maintain some control over the situation that really they have no control. This creates an internal core of shame ... a deep, false belief that says

I'm bad, no good, not enough, wrong, a mistake, inadequate, and unlovable. We made them wonderful and created a fantasy bond that said that they were really there for us; that is why today we choose people who really can't be there for us either.

Believing we are bad drives us to look for validation, "okayness", security, value, and love outside of ourselves in someone else. We carefully hid our real bad self from others with an act because they would not love us if they really knew us (just like our parents).

It never works because the little child part of us chooses over and over again, someone just like momma or daddy who wouldn't or can't give either, and who will abuse, abandon, or neglect us. So, here we are stuck in repetitive compulsive relationships that never work

I have read this essay many times and learned something new every time I allow it's wisdom to inspire me. Now, I will repeat this part of her essay, but include my thoughts. For clarity, her writings will be in *italics*.

Our parents did the best they could; they did not intend to hurt us.

I do not think any parent looks at a child and says, "I am going to screw up this kid." Yet no parent raised a child perfectly, and children suffer the harmful effects of imperfect parents.

We come from our mothers' wombs, where all life requirements were met completely and absolutely. Suddenly, we are born, and we are utterly dependent on outside resources, starting with our mother's milk. In the natural state of being, very dependent, children latch on to any perception of reality offered by their caregivers. A child's very survival depends upon accepting this truth as absolute. Children naturally believe without question and absorb knowledge at an incredible rate; since there is no other frame of reference; they believe their parental reality, true or false.

I know I abused my children, not intentionally but from my own disconnection, my limited ability to express the love I felt, and my destructive thoughts, behaviors and coping skills. I gave them the best I knew but, in reality, my love was not enough. I had to learn how to love.

When my children were teenagers, I sat them down to parent them and tell them how to live life in the best way I knew how. Teenagers can spot hypocrisy a mile away and here I was telling them how to cope when they witnessed the shambles of my own life and how I was living. When I would try to talk to them, their eyes would roll and glaze over and then their ears would close. I did what most parents do in these circumstances: I got louder! They referred to these little talks as the "lecture". With improved coping skills forged through my midlife crisis, I now listen first and do not control, and I allow these now adult children to come to their own conclusions about what they want for their lives.

Life's normal progression is from a dependent child to a fully mature adult. A child's reality, provided by these giants called parents, becomes their own. Life's journey into maturity starts with believing everything you've been told and then evolving into healthy maturity where we can challenge childhood learning and develop new perceptions tempered by personal introspection, additional wisdom, and experience. Mature adults gravitate toward new values and understandings, not just rehashing and blind acceptance of past patterns and previous learning. This is an ongoing process and maturity demands lifelong learners.

Exercise 20

- Where did your parents fail you? What emotional scars do you carry from their imperfect parenting skills?

- Where have you failed as a parent? What emotional scars do your children carry from your imperfect parenting skills? Remember, you are not a perfect parent but a fallible human being doing the best you know how at this moment...just like your parents.

You might be a Chaos Person if...
you are so vain you think it was your spark
that set off the Big Bang.

Joanne T.

They had injuries from their past that kept them from being able to be there for us emotionally, to parent us in the way a little child needs ... they abused, neglected, and/or abandoned us: physically, emotionally, and/or spiritually.

While growing up, children witness life through the low-level eyes of youth; they are always looking upward toward the giants surrounding and controlling them. Children have empty erasable white boards upon which big people write indelibly imprinted messages into their tender subconscious minds. Maturity requires a series of changes of letting go of how Mommy and Daddy thought and lived into new realities based upon additional learning. Letting go of what does not work becomes quite difficult, for it is contrary to a child's natural learning through close bonding with parents. Sadly, some childhood learning comes from wounds deep within us where we store these scars in our shame closet.

> *"There is an expiry date on blaming your parents*
> *for steering you in the wrong direction;*
> *the moment you are old enough to take the wheel,*
> *responsibility lies with you."*
> J. K. Rowling

Exercise - 21

What do you wish to erase from your white board?

You might be a Chaos Person if...
your definition of intimacy
is a joint checking account.

Joanne T.

This childhood wound causes codependency.

Codependency is a learned set of behaviors, thought processes, and habits. When combined together, they fit a very loose definition. All people exhibit these traits to some degree, but some of us allow them to dictate our relationships with others and ourselves. These coping skills are used to attempt to make our way through this world and relate to others. Usually these traits include control, manipulation, and passive aggressive methods of conflict resolution. When taken to the extreme, they become pathological and are roadblocks to effectively sharing love with others.

Wounded parents often unintentionally inflict pain and suffering on their children and these childhood wounds causes a laundry list of mal-adaptive behaviors commonly called codependency. These habits re-strict people to love-limiting relationships causing much unhappiness and distress.

Dan Smith, EdD, MFT describes Codependency as:

> "The condition or fact of being codependent; specifi-cally: tendency to place the needs and wants of others first and to the exclusion of acknowledging one's own continued investment of self-esteem in the ability to control both oneself and others anxiety and boundary distortions relating to intimacy and separation difficul-ty expressing feelings excessive worry how others may respond to one's feelings undue fear of being hurt and/or rejected by others self-esteem dependent on ap-proval by others tendency to ignore own values and at-tempt to adhere to the values of others."

Codependency is not included in the Diagnostic and Statistical Manual, the bible of the mental health profession. This book describes the vari-ous mental health symptoms and provides universal diagnostic codes. Codependency is a real problem, though its description does not meet the strict standards required for inclusion of this prestigious reference book. Although not recognized by the DMS, it is much of the basis of the treatment provided by most mental health counselors. If we want to improve, we have to first recognize our own maladaptive coping skills, called codependency, then change.

When I started focusing on changing me, I read a wonderful book, *Codependency No More* by Melody Beattie; I wished I'd written it. After finishing the book, I copied the list of the behaviors she described, highlighting my traits in yellow. When I reviewed the significant traits, I had highlighted most of them. At that moment, I knew where I needed to start and what I needed to change. Thank you, Melody. If you were to read her book perhaps the same clarity will be yours.

Exercise - 22

Review each of Dan H. Smith's codependency symptoms. Which ones do you identify with? Write a little about how these traits have affected your life.

> Tendency to place the needs and wants of others first, to the exclusion of acknowledging one's own

> Continued investment of self-esteem in the ability to control both oneself and others

> Anxiety and boundary distortions relating to intimacy and separation

Difficulty expressing feelings

Excessive worry how others may respond to one's feelings

Undue fear of being hurt and/or rejected by others

Self-esteem dependent on approval by others

Tendency to ignore own values and attempt to adhere to the values of others.

You might be a Chaos Person if...
you're such a narcissist,
you can't look in a mirror
without getting excited.

Joanne T.

> *Parents (or our major caregivers), who are hurt them-*
> *selves and are hiding their own feelings and pain from*
> *themselves, are not real and present to themselves;*
> *therefore, they cannot be present and available for*
> *their children.*

As a parent who raised his children in dysfunction, I know the parental wounds my children received were not intentional; often they were my best expression of love, sometimes coming out sideways, not as I intended. I think this makes the wound even deeper. Here is their daddy who loves them, but his love comes packaged in pain. This creates confusion between love and pain. Unless recognized, this pattern is inflicted upon the next generation. The greater the pain associated with love, the more likely a person is to be attracted to others who will inflict this pain…for isn't this what love is? Hurt people tend to hurt other people.

Exercise - 23

Do you also confuse love and pain? How has this confusion affect your life?

You might be a Chaos Person if...
you look so care-worn you make
Abraham Lincoln look happy.

When my youngest sister divorced her husband, a man I loved, I judged her fiercely and condemned her decision. She then told me about her confusion between love and pain; this dichotomy is what she was used to growing up. This made so much sense to me and I commemorated this discussion by personalizing it in the poem, Knows So Well.

Knows So Well

My young child's
terrified cry
then soft sobs
of exhausted fright.
This child which lives
within my being,
abandoned long ago
locked in a closet
dark and secret place
deep within my soul.

Pain was all he knew.
I told him
it
was
love.

Real love he did not know.
And now he searches
for what he knows best ...
the familiar
the ... pain.

He seeks the pain
he knows so well ...
and he
calls
it ...
love.

A client of mine, who came in because of her divorce, told me: "I found my husband under a rock. I took him home and watered and fed him in order for him to be good enough for me." Here is a perfect example of a woman confusing love and pain. She chose someone "...under a rock" who inflicts pain on her, then calls it love. The question she needs to ask herself to begin her healing process is: "What caused me to look under rocks in the first place?"

Clara, a friend of mine, metaphorically described her last relationship: "I was happily swimming all by myself when I was attracted to a water moccasin. It was so pretty, I petted it, took it home with me, and then he bit me." When I asked her, "Why did you find poisonous snakes so attractive, and didn't you know snakes bite?" She replied, "Well, he promised he would shed his skin and I thought my love could help him!"

If you are looking for love under rocks or bringing home water moccasins, you might be confusing love and pain.

Exercise - 24

Have you been looking under rocks for love? Bring any water moccasins home lately? What happen when the moccasin did not shed his skin as promised? Do you think your *picker* may be broken?

You might be a Chaos Person if...
growing up you always wanted to be somebody.
Now that you are grown up you wish
you had been more specific.

Joanne T.

> *Most often, they (parents) have some form of addictive*
> *or compulsive behavior to cover their own pain. This*
> *causes them to abuse, neglect, or abandon us in thou-*
> *sands of different and sometimes subtle ways.*

People who are hurting, hurt other people. Hurt parents feel the pain, and hiding from its effects may be the only way they know how to deal with the abandonment and hurts they received as a child and may still experience today. When I started to understand myself, I discovered the wounds I received growing up. Now armed with this realization, instead of blaming my parents, I wanted to know what my parents experienced. What were their pains, their wounds? What kept them from being there for me, as I needed?

Eventually, my Dad and I shared this deep understanding. In these profound exchanges, we got honest, and I actually grieved his approaching death with him before he died. When he passed away, I had nothing left I needed to say to him and, because of our honesty; I started my grieving with him. I am so glad I was able to experience this with my Dad. From this experience, I recommend talking to your loved ones about death; say what you need to express before they die. If you have this intimate conversation before they leave, you will be glad you did and their passing can be a healing experience for both you and your loved one.

I tried to get to know my mother. I did not know what was behind her smiling face and her obsessive desire to focus on other people's happiness. On my last attempt, she said with such determination, "I can't talk about that." I knew right then conversation was over. This one sentence was the degree to which I was able to understand her. She went to her grave with me not really knowing who she was. I know what she did, the people who loved her, and the love she gave to me, but I did not know my mother as I wanted to. She was hiding her pain and heartbreaks behind a mask, not trusting that anyone could possibility love her without her protective cover. Sad.

Understanding my pain gave me insight into the hurt I inflicted on those I love. A big part of my motivation for writing this book was to apologize for what I inflicted upon them. Maybe my relatives will read this and gain knowledge I did not have; thus maybe preventing them from passing on my dysfunction, I hope.

Exercise - 25

How did your parents express their own wounds? Did you experience their wounds being unintentionally inflicted upon you? What emotional scars do you still carry from childhood?

You might be a Chaos Person if...
you decided the answer to your weight
problem is to move to somewhere
where there is less gravity.

Joanne T.

We, as little ones, could not see our parents (our Gods)...

Our parents were our first gods. If parents are loving, nurturing, and kind, this becomes the child's definition of the creator. If parents were controlling, angry, and manipulative, then this becomes their definition. Knowing sets us free to establish our own definition, free to have our mature relationship with the Creative Force, not necessarily one based upon the image created by Mom and Dad. As the adult, you get to review your relationship with Creation and make your own definition. This freedom allows you to develop a God of *YOUR understanding*.

Before doing a lot of my own *Thumb Work*, I did what my religion dictated. I desperately tried to live and believe as my parents understood. I fervently did what the church books told me. Even with this intense focus, I did not feel very close to my Creator; I thought I heard His voice but it was distant and fleeting. When I went inside of me and found and claimed the gift I was given called "me" then this connection became real. Religions are not the problem, but it is hard to feel close to a Creator-in-the-sky until one goes inside themselves and finds the spark of the divine living within us all.

> *"...the only constant in life is change...*
> *the only question is how you are going*
> *to change and how you are going*
> *to try to make other things change."*
> Wilbert Rideau

Exercise - 26

Describe your parents. What adjectives would you use for your parents and compare this description and your current definition of how you view your god?

What do you want to believe about your definition of god? Note: I purposely used the small "g" as different people see their creator differently and I do not wish to inflict some burden of another's definition upon you.

> ***You might be a Chaos Person if...***
> you are smart enough to check
> with his former girlfriends
> but discount their advice to run.

Joanne T.

We, as little ones, could not see our parents (our Gods) as bad; therefore, we decided that we were bad. Children do not have a frame of reference to judge parents and by taking responsibility for their parents, they maintain some control over the situation that really they have no control.

Children experiencing grief from their parents' divorce where they are powerless to prevent this loss of stability from happening, very often think the reason Mommy and Daddy broke up was "I've been a bad kid." This belief gives them some degree of control, some power when they feel powerlessness over something not belonging to them, about a situation they did not cause and cannot control.

Consider a man who had a series of unsuccessful relationships with women who he tends to treat as objects, not people. During self-discovery, he remembered a childhood incident and the very subtle message he received and incorporated into his subconscious. One day, his mother had an argument with her husband on the telephone. The mother was very upset and cried. After she hung up the phone, she turned to her young impressionable son and burdened him with her emotional pain when she said, "Kiss Mommy and make Mommy happy again." This child did and magically restored mother's happiness.

This example is so typical of the vulnerability of children. When any adults: parents, school teachers, or the Cub Scout Master use children to unload emotional burdens and make them part of emotional trauma, children are ill-equipped to handle the weight of adult issues. This particular child brought this perception into adulthood; he learned from Mom he could magically make women feel better with just his kiss. Because of this small incident hidden in the dark recesses of his mind, he thought he had this power to change women's moods with his powerful kiss. It did not work in any of his relationships but he kept on trying.

Isn't it strange the effect an innocent comment had on this man? All adults have childhood wounds; some are small scars and some are very large and gaping wounds. Just having these wounds does not excuse anyone's behavior; realizing what happened and the effect it has on you today allows for understanding. With this awareness, transmitting this abuse to another is not necessary.

Remember, no matter how bad our childhood, we are responsible for our own behavior, or as my Reality Therapist, Gene Snellings, taught in his counseling classes: "It's too bad your dad is on death row, your mother sleeps around, your brother is in the mafia, your sister is a prostitute …*you don't steal cars…Bubba!"* What Gene is saying, as adults we are totally responsible for how we live our lives and the degree of happiness we enjoy regardless of how we were raised.

I had a young client who experienced a sexual assault. After listening to her horrific story, I gave her the Mood Chart and requested her to paint a rainbow of the emotions she was now feeling. She told me, "Anger, disgust, ashamed, embarrassed, humiliated, and hurt." I then repeated these feelings back to her to acknowledge I heard and for this little girl to hear her own feelings bounced back to her ears and know that someone has heard her.

I pondered aloud to her about my curiosity regarding one of her feelings… *shame*. "Tell me, did you do anything you should feel ashamed about?" After thinking about the events, she realized she did nothing wrong. I confirmed this by saying, "You could walk down the street buck naked and no one has the right to attack you." Then I asked her, "Do you tend to own emotions rightfully belonging to others?"

She hesitated then nodded, so I said, "Does the shame belong to you or rightfully belong to the attacker?" A smile came over her face and she pulled her shoulders back and responded, "Him."

Exercise - 27

If we are not aware, it is so easy to own the emotions and/or behavior belonging to another. What areas of your life have you taken responsibility for someone else's emotions and/or behavior?

You might be a Chaos Person if...
someone knocks you down
on the street and you get up apologizing.

Joanne T.

> *This creates an internal core of shame ... a deep, false*
> *belief that says I'm bad, no good, not enough, wrong, a*
> *mistake, inadequate, and unlovable.*

These beliefs are the necessary materials for building a large and dark shame closet deep within us. Remember…these beliefs are false, regardless of personal history, regardless of abuse by family, and regardless of abandonment by people once relied upon and loved.

Shame is a powerful feeling. There is a tremendous difference between making a mistake and believing you are a mistake. One client struggled with this concept and told me, "If I don't see myself as being a mistake then it is I who must take responsibility and I am not ready to accept that."

Remember despite how you might have been raised, the truth of it is…you are good enough…now. This attitude of *being good enough* is an automatic shame reducer.

Exercise - 28

What shame do you feel? What is lurking in the deep recesses of your shame closet? What are you fearful of bringing to the light of day?

You might be a Chaos Person if...
you don't take "no" for an answer,
because "maybe" will do.

Joanne T.

We made them wonderful and created a fantasy bond that said that they were really there for us; that is why today we choose people who really can't be there for us either. Believing we are bad drives us to look for validation, "okayness," security, value, and love outside of ourselves in someone else.

Children innately know their parents stand between them and horrible unimaginable doom. This is a natural fear of what would happen if these giants called Mommy and Daddy would ever leave. Picture baby ducks. As they hatch, they latch onto their mother and follow her. In nature, their life depends on this rigid compliance to duck-norms because this blind obedience is the only protection little ducks have from a hungry fox. Children want to please their parents and latch onto them hoping not to be the duckling left behind. When children experience hurt and pain from parents...*this is bad enough but whatever you do Momma duck, do not leave.*

Like the baby ducks, fear of abandonment is a natural survival mechanism requiring children to stay close to their parental protectors. There is considerable damage caused when fear of abandonment controls an adult. In a love relationship, this fear is now transferred onto someone else.

Exercise - 29

Scan yourself for your feelings of abandonment. Is this abandonment interfering with your ability to love? How is this affecting your trust level?

You might be a Chaos Person if...
during your divorce you experienced
a terrible custody battle.
You ex-wife doesn't want you back
neither does your mother.

Joanne T.

We carefully hid our real bad self from others with an
act because they would not love us if they really knew
us (just like our parents).

If I am real and this is who I am…then…if you reject me, I could not
stand this rejection, so I cannot ever let you in to know the real me, just
like my mother. In reality, if I do not know the real me, who I really
am…how can I be vulnerable to others?

Exercise - 30

Do you wear a mask? Are you fearful of being honest? How does wearing a mask (your fear of being honest) interfere with your significant
relationship?

You might be a Chaos Person if…
it's been many years and you're
still grieving over the death
of the frog you dissected
in high school biology class.

Joanne T.

It never works because the little child part of us choos-
es over and over again, someone just like momma or
daddy who wouldn't or can't give either, and who will
abuse, abandon, or neglect us. So, here we are stuck in
repetitive compulsive relationships that never work.

People are attracted to their psychological twin, drawn to what we know. If chaos is our normal, guess what excites us? Someone who is normal is similar…just like us. If Mommy found Daddy "under a rock" and spent her energies trying to change him, this becomes the pattern you grew up with. If Mommy was a water moccasin and you witness Daddy's pain and hurt when the she-snake refused to change her skin as promised, you are more than likely to repeat this pattern.

Picture two people who each are holding a slice of Swiss cheese, this cheese has holes in it. In this example, each hole represents a wound. Since all children suffer some abuse, abandonment, and hurt, all people have holes in their Swiss cheese. When we share our hole-filled cheese with someone, we need to have close alignment for attraction to occur. When their magnitude of holes somewhat matches ours…well, romance begins. If the other person does not have the same magnitude of holes (wounds) as ours, they reject us and the tears of rebuff begin. If they have more holes than what we consider normal (like ours) we reject them and give them the "It's not you…it's me" speech.

As Joanne T. said, "Our parents did the best they could…" Accepting this realization frees us from " …wanting them to change so we can be okay."

Our parenting skills are probably similar to our experience growing up…some of it good and some not so good. However, it now belongs to us…it is our choice to continue the pattern or make improvements. Reading this book proves you do not wish to inflict the damage done to you upon your children or anyone else in your life.

Exercise - 31

How difficult would it be to accept your parents as doing "…the best they could"?

With the eyes of your own maturity, where have you witnessed when your parents, "…were hurt themselves and are hiding their own feelings and pain from themselves, are not real and present to themselves?" How did they express this pain?

All children experience abandonment, from a little to a lot. Everything about parenting seems to be an emergency. At today's frantic pace, earning a living, cooking supper, and getting junior to soccer practice takes priority and we sometimes neglect our childrens real needs. Think about your childhood: where did your parents abandon you, failed to listen, controlled you, forced you to conform to their demands and definitions, or many other subtle ways you missed out on what you deserved but did not receive? How is this affecting you today?

What would happen if you forgave your parents for their imperfect parenting skills, the abuse, and the abandonment you received?

You might be a Chaos Person if...
you're so defiant, you wear green
every day of the year,
except St. Patrick's Day.

Healing –

Here is part two of the essay. It needs separation from the first part which she described the problem. Now Joanne T. talks about healing.

> *Healing comes from seeing the truth, telling the truth, and coming to believe the truth. It is not about blaming our parents for that would keep us a victim, caught still wanting them to change so we would be okay. It is about having the truth set us free. When we face the truth, we are free; free to forgive ourselves and see we are valuable, wonderful, and loveable even when we make mistakes. We are free to forgive our parents; free to find new relationships or improve the old; relationships built on the truth that we are God's precious children and deserve love ... building on the present not a reenactment of the past chaos.*

Notice how Joanne T. suggests maybe it is time to break many of our family dysfunctional habits by "...*telling the truth*." This decision involves us dropping our *victim* mentality and becoming honest.

Exercise – 32

Would breaking these habits and doing what dear Joanne suggests help you in your quest for serenity? How would it help? What habits would you have to break and how are you going to break them?

You might be a Chaos Person if...
you declare your yard a sovereign nation,
declare war on the United States,
anticipating losing but
hoping for reconstruction funds.

Forgiveness –

"The only way out of the labyrinth of suffering is to forgive."
John Green

The final part of the study Joanne T. provided us is all about forgiveness.

> **ONE CAUTION:** *Do not jump to forgiveness before you take the time to see the truth about what happened to you and to feel the feelings associated with those events; sometimes those feelings are locked deep within our psyches. Feel the pain of the childhood abuse, abandonment, and/or neglect; feel the grief about the loss of your innocence, of what you needed and did not receive, these are the healing feelings. The hiding of these feelings causes our addiction, compulsivity, and codependency. Tell the truth, feel the feelings, grieve the grief, and then with your permission allow the forgiveness to happen ... this is freedom."* Give yourself permission to understand before jumping into the magic healing pool of forgiveness.

All people have experienced disappointments, hurts, and injustice. Everyone has lost something, someone, or felt unfairly treated. This is part of life. Remember, "Life is hard" and "Life ain't fair." Once a person realizes those two wonderful insights and acknowledges their deepest, darkest resentments, healing has an opportunity to happen.

Forgiveness is not about the other person, the #@*&!!$# person who "done you wrong." Forgiveness is an inside job; it is about you. This does not mean you will forget the injustice or loss, but with forgiveness it mean you will no longer allow the crushing experience to control your life.

I had a friend named Charlie. Notice I said had..."had" being the operative word. Charlie missed his child support payments because of his chronic unemployment and called me requesting my help for he was serving a 30-day sentence. He wanted me to pick his car up from his attorney's office and take it to his house. Once I agreed to this minor service, he asked me to pay his rent and a few other bills. I said I would, after all Charlie was a friend, right?

When I picked up his car, I discovered it barely started and had terrible brakes. Being Charlie's friend, I had the car tuned and the brakes fixed. I then paid his bills and picked him up at midnight when he was released. The next day he came to my office and signed a promissory note for the full amount, promising to pay $50.00 per month.

Several months went by and Charlie faithfully paid his note and then, guess what happened? You got it. He stopped paying. He didn't respond to my requests and then I found out he had bought a brand-new computer. You can understand why I copped a large resentment. I could feel this resentment weighing me down. I knew I was paying a price for holding on to this injustice from my now ex-friend Charlie.

Fortunately, I had a group of enlightened friends who provided a wonderful insight when I shared this burden. When I finished my tale of woe, a man in the group asked, "Do you want to know what I do when I have resentment and want to let go of it?" Upon receiving my enthusiastic "Yes," he told me his experience: "When I have resentment and wish to let it go, instead of dwelling on how this person wronged me, I change my thoughts. I start thinking good thoughts about this person." What a novel idea. When I returned home I put a picture of my ex-friend Charlie on my bulletin board. Then every morning when I viewed his photograph, I said aloud, "I wish you well, Charlie." Did my resentment go away? It sure did. Did I get my money back? No, I did not. Had I not changed my attitude, I would still have this resentment restricting my happiness, plus…no money. By letting go of this resentment, all I am out is the money. By letting go, I regained my peace. I am so glad I had this experience to learn this wonderful lesson: Think positive thoughts about those who have harmed you, hard to do…yes. The greater the injustice, the harder this is to do.

Then a second lesson appeared unexpectedly. Follow my thought process: did I set myself up for failure? What I did was loan money to someone who was in jail for non-support of his family and then I expected him to pay me back. Where was my reasoning ability? I was a people pleaser; I wanted so much for people to like me. With this out-of-control mindset, I ignored my better judgment and invested money in a dry well. With my best intentions and my compulsive desire to be liked, I owned Charlie's problem. I did not allow him to be responsible for his behavior, and I paid the price.

Exercise - 33

What did you learn from my example about my "friend" Charlie? Do you have some resentment you need to get rid of? What are you going to do about your resentment…hold on to it or let it go?

You might be a Chaos Person if...
your idea of getting dressed
is deciding what mask to hide behind.

True forgiveness has three distinct parts.

Part One is saying the words, admitting your error, and asking for forgiveness. Although this is a desirable part of the forgiveness process, by itself it is not enough. Many people suing a company for a perceived wrong have told me…"Yes, I'd like to be compensated, but what I really would like is an apology."

Part Two is perhaps the hardest. When making an amends, you have to become willing to listen to how your behavior affects the other person. This takes broad shoulders and not everyone is willing to endure the realization of how their behavior caused another's pain. If your self-esteem is shallow, hearing someone criticizing your behavior is difficult at best. I hope you take the opportunity hereafter to listen to those you hurt. When you listen to the aggrieved person, a large part of the healing process has begun, sometimes called closure.

Are you ready to make amends? Are you now willing to listen to how your behavior made them feel?

Part Three is also difficult: change behavior. If the behavior is not changed and the behavior continues to inflict pain, all the original forgiveness gained is lost, becomes invalidated, and the original pain is then exacerbated.

Are you ready to change your behavior?

Making amends is not only saying the words but also being willing to listen to how your behavior caused another's pain, and then the really hard part…changing behavior.

"The weak can never forgive.
Forgiveness is the
attribute of the strong."
Mahatma Gandhi

Part V – Antidotes -Dysfunctional Habits

It is one thing to know about your dysfunctional habits but quite another to change them. There are suggestions in this section to explore those habits you wish to change, and to begin the process of healing. Once you realize your behavior has hurt the people you love and has contributed to your feelings of shame, depression, and isolation, here are some suggestions to begin the long and arduous process of changing and becoming all you wish you could be, claiming your magnificence.

This is not a quick fix, one-size-fits-all solution. Sitting on the hot seat of change requires much courage, patience, and persistence. Using the Antidotes is really changing our immature and dysfunctional methods of loving into a much more mature ability to have successful relationships. When we put aside bad habits and remove the barriers, we allow what we keenly feel to flow freely, for…*love is not enough.*

Antidote to Don't Talk

*"I just feel compelled to continue to be transparent.
It just really levels the playing field and
eradicates the shame that I have,
or that one might have, about being human."*
Alanis Morissette

Everyone needs a place to be honest. The Twelve Steps community has an expression, "We are as sick as our secrets." With the *Don't Talk* Habit firmly in place, we dare not be honest, for our secrets are locked deep within us where they fester in the dark, turn cancerous, and add to the clutter in our Shame Closet.

Researcher Dr. Brené Brown has studied the power of shame; these intensely painful feelings suggest: "Shame emphasizes what is wrong with us. It has an inward focus, which leads to feeling poorly about ourselves, rather than simply the actions we have taken. Malignant shame, the core effect of addiction, can be treacherous, dangerous and even lethal to the addict as well as to family members and others." Dr. Brown says shame is "…lethal…deadly"…and "…we are swimming in it…" You don't have to be affected by addiction to be drowning in shame.

Some people exhibit this habit, hiding their shame by being stoic; you cannot read their faces, they're the strong silent type. Some hide in histrionic behaviors becoming the focal point of controversy by reacting in highly emotional outbursts. Others hide from being real by filling the air with words; the more words they throw out, the less actual communication happens and they are left with only an illusion of connection. This is the intimacy they so ardently seek but with these coping skills find so elusive. These are several examples of wounded people so afraid to connect with others and so frighten of rejection that they surround themselves in a protective cocoon of non-communication, a highly developed protective shield keeping secrets in and intimacy out.

If you want an antidote to the *Don't Talk* Habit then as trite as it is…you must talk. However, it is important you choose your place to talk. To break the *Don't Talk* Habit, find an accepting environment. If you feel judged in your chosen place, or if this is similar to your childhood experience with your family, label places of judgment as non-safe. You need others who will listen, accept you as you are, not to judge you and not attempt to "FIX" you. You are perfectly capable of "fixing" yourself. All you need is a safe place to be understood.

Here are several suggestions and depending on what you may be dealing with, at least one is suitable for you:

- Church Priest/Clergy
- Divorce Recovery Group
- Rape Crisis Center
- Mental health Counselor
- Support Groups

With many clients, I encourage their attendance in a Twelve Step Program. They sometimes shudder with the thought of being open in a group of strangers and they recoil, saying, "I am more comfortable with solving my problems directly with you," or "I'm not a group person." These are all places to hide for it is indeed scary to violate the *Don't Talk* Habit especially in a crowd...what if Mother found out, and what would she say?

What always amazes me when I attend a Twelve Step group is the wisdom in those meetings. Picture a room full of people who, by their own admission, have some identifiable addiction or compulsive behavior...wounded people. Here, they share their darkest secrets in a structured environment conducive to honesty. Just by entering the doors, they are acknowledging their desire to have a better and happier life. With tongue in cheek, I jokingly tell people, "Don't have an addiction? Get one. You'll love working a Twelve Step program!"

Here is a list of some of the Twelve Step Programs; maybe one is for you.

- Al-Anon
- Alcohol Anonymous
- Codependent Anonymous
- Compulsive Gamblers Anonymous
- Narcotics Anonymous
- Overeater's Anonymous
- Sex Addicts Anonymous

A strange feature of the *Don't Talk* Habit is the connection to listening. In order to connect with others and break this habit, one must also become a good listener. One of the disciplines that participants learn in a group environment, such as a Twelve Step Program, is listening skills. One member of AA told me he had to learn to listen because, "…my life depended upon it."

When you attend a self-help meeting, you do not want others to judge you. With Twelve Step groups, members listen with acceptance. Having others not only listen to you, but try their best to understand your world, is powerful enough and seldom found elsewhere. This marvelous gift, coupled with an atmosphere of acceptance instead of judgment, is what makes "these rooms" a place of healing. Here, members accept you, as you are at that moment, and this acceptance becomes a powerful antidote to the *Don't Talk* Habit.

> *"Nothing brings down walls*
> *as surely as acceptance."*
> Deepak Chopra

Exercise - 34

Find a place, group, or individual where you can be honest and then put yourself in the place of healing. After a while, you will feel comfortable talking about that which could not be spoken of before.

What would you have to give up? What would you have to change if you started attending a self-help meeting? Would your attendance require you to give up some essential part of who you are? What do you think you may gain from the experience?

> ***You might be a Chaos Person if...***
> your expectations are so low
> your ideal date is someone who
> doesn't fall drunk into his spaghetti.

Antidote to Don't Trust

"(They) drew a circle that shut me out –
heretic, rebel, a thing to flout.
But love and I had the wit to win:
we drew a circle and took (them) in."
Edwin Markham, adapted.

The scariest two words couples often hear is "Let's talk." When said in this manner, all of our insecurities pop up and the difficult choices then present themselves, become intimate or hide. How can a person break the *Don't Talk* Habit when that person does not trust?

Recently a client told me, "I am very scared about being honest with you." Instead of taking her comment personally, I congratulated her on her honesty for it took a leap of faith and tremendous courage for her to begin breaking the *Don't Trust* Habit. For this young woman, when she revealed her fear of getting honest with me, she took a giant step in her progress.

Breaking the *Don't Trust* Habit requires a desire to trust, a place of acceptance, and a great deal of courage to get out of one's comfort zone and violate the *Don't Talk* Habit... reaching out...then trusting.

The strange part about a person's lack of trust is that it often comes from not trusting themselves. I've always recognized a little voice within me, but prior to doing *Thumb Work*, I'd often ignore it. Even when this inner voice spoke to me loud and in uncertain terms, I did not trust it, often to my peril. When you journey inwardly exploring yourself, a sense of personal trust begins. As this happens, your attention to this little voice becomes sharper and you begin to trust. Some people call this little voice the "God Voice" and some call it the "Little Professor", but whatever you call your little voice, it has a high degree of accuracy.

"Whatever you can do, or
dream you can, begin it.
Johann Wolfgang Goethe

In graduate school at Texas A&M, I had two vivid examples of my little voice speaking to me and they both happened exactly the same way, but at two different times and with two different people. In both instances, at the beginning of a semester, I watched a student walk into class about 10 minutes late for the first session. Each time, their tardiness caused a disruption in the class. I had never met these two tardy people before, but on both occasions, when I first saw them, my little voice said, "Trust." Later, after getting to know both people, they became my good friends and I discovered both had already done a significant amount work on themselves. One was a recovering alcoholic who had been in 12 Step many years. The other had her trial of fire precipitated by the infidelity of her husband, and afterwards she entered therapy making giant strides in her own self-love journey. What I sensed about them both was their peacefulness. Had I not had my own serenity, I probably would have missed their calmness. Because my antenna was in tune, I now could listen to my intuitive voice, something I had so often ignored before. Had I not been aware, these deep friendships might not have happened. I am so glad I was able to sense their calmness; I am so glad I then trusted my Little Professor.

Serenity is available to obtain for everyone but requires considerable work. *Thumb Work* is never easy but always rewarding. In order to break the *Don't Trust Habit,* listen to your own *Little Professor,* trust yourself by being *trustworthy to yourself.* As Don Ruiz writes in his book, *The Four Agreements*, "Be impeccable with your word." As best you can, live up to your promises, especially the ones you declare to yourself. Honoring your word is the fiber from which trust is built. To break this habit, step out of your norm and begin to trust.

> *"Trust yourself. You know more*
> *than you think you do."*
> Benjamin Spock

Exercise - 35

Do you listen to your little voice? Describe when you listened to it and had positive results. Describe some times when you did not listen, creating a mess.

To break the *Don't Trust* Habit, start becoming more aware of your inner voice. Had you been ignoring it before? What is it telling you now?

Antidote to Don't Feel

"If we don't change the direction soon,
we'll end up where we are heading."
Unknown

As children, when tucked in at night, many of us felt scared about what was under our beds. Something would surely get us if we stepped out of our warm bed onto the cold floor. If we do not understand, acknowledge, and correctly use our emotions, we fear their power and they become our monsters under the bed.

People who are unwilling to talk about deep personal issues do not trust their own emotions. The antidote, you already know it…the Mood Chart. Make a copy of this chart and begin to speak the feeling language. When growing up with others who are not emotionally honest, using the feeling language is like speaking a foreign language; it is very difficult in the beginning. Expressing the rainbow of feelings flowing through your soul may be awkward at first, but with willingness and practice, you will be successful. To break the *Don't Feel* Habit, start with acknowledging the five basic feeling words: mad, glad, sad, fear, and hurt. Then, when comfortable, use the rest of the many feelings listed on the Mood Chart.

If I kicked you very hard in the shins, what would you immediately say? That is, what you would say to me *before you cussed me out.* You would say "Ouch"…right? (In this exercise, I kicked you in the shins, it hurt, and your natural response would be to say "Ouch.") Why can't we use this same feedback method to convey the pain when emotionally hurt? This is a simple but powerful way of being honest about the hurt you feel. What would happen if you conveyed your emotional pain to others by saying, "Ouch"? Would this be a good method to begin becoming emotionally honest? You are comfortable expressing physical pain, so can you also become comfortable expressing emotional pain?

Your emotions are a navigation tool, your radar set. If not used, you will be like the Titanic and run into the icebergs of life. When you do not use your radar set and ignore your emotions, you will sink many times.

Exercise - 36

Use the Mood Chart to express your feelings. Paint a rainbow of emotions for others to understand you. Ask your significant others to use the Mood Chart to express themselves. Before you begin this exercise, list your feelings from the Mood Chart about getting honest with those in your family…what do you feel?

You might be a Chaos Person if...
the only way you know of getting rid
of a bad mood is to pass it on!

Antidote to Don't Change

Change is like cooking an egg for breakfast. Shattering the shell begins a chain reaction; the egg will never be the same. The cooking process transforms the egg; then after eating it, the body changes the egg once again into fuel. Breaking and cooking eggs is always messy and so is the change process.

If you were facing the possible death from a medical condition and your doctor said you needed to radically alter your lifestyle to live, would you do it? Most people would emphatically shake their heads, yes. Heart attack, stroke, and cancer victims are examples of people facing shortened life spans unless they change their lives. All people facing life or death decisions involving drastic lifestyle changes have tremendous odds for failure—nine out of ten return to their old destructive behavior within two years. Most vow to change but only a few succeed. Why? The hard part about the soft part of change is breaking the *Don't Change* Habit.

Valero Energy hired me to be their "culture change catalyst" for their plant in Krotz Springs, Louisiana. In this capacity, I was the tip of the point of the arrow of change. I told the plant manager, "In performing this function, I'm going to be the needle, and you're the doctor, and together we're going puncture this infected boil. In this process, we'll get pus all over the place, but this wound will be healed." This proved an accurate description of what happened.

In the middle of the *pus stage* of this operation, a very large operator looked down at me and said in a deep and menacing voice, "We have a new nickname for you." When I questioned what was the latest in a series of names inflicted on me (some of which were humorous and some quite unrepeatable), he simply said, "Troublemaker!" I knew then we were on the right track, for as my friend, Bob Pries says, "Change is messy."

Dr. Dean Ornish, founder of the Preventative Medicine Research Institute, realizes the importance of the emotional component coexisting with the data driving the change. "Providing health information is important but not always sufficient," he says. "We also need to bring in the psychological, emotional, and spiritual dimensions so often ignored." The reason lifestyle changes have such a dismal record, Ornish thinks, is motivation by fear is not enough to sustain the change. He thinks death is too frightening to think about, and denial is a trick our brain successfully plays on us. Change will not successfully happen unless the emotional component is solved.

Consider the disease of alcoholism as an example of this dynamic. When I encourage my alcoholic clients to attend Alcoholics Anonymous, I tell them, "I do not want you to quit drinking." They look at me in amazement for this is not the message they expected. I continue with this explanation: "The only requirement for AA is a *desire* to quit drinking; does any part of you have this desire?" Most shake their head in reluctant agreement not wanting to be caught in a verbal trap. I then continue: "And until you find something better than alcohol, do not quit drinking. Alcohol has been your mistress for many years; it is your developed coping skill allowing you to hide from the pain of living. AA is not about alcohol; it is about a new and better way of living. You will not know if this way of living is better for you until you give AA a try."

Most alcoholics do not quit drinking out of fear of imprisonment, death, or significant loss; their denial system is ingrained, protecting their addiction. In the accepting protection of the recovery community, such as AA, participants begin to connect with their long hidden emotions, begin to think differently, and then to talk about their own "monsters under the bed." This type of group allows people to be honest and this experience reduces denial creating the space for recovery to begin. Here, they discover coping skills that work better than drinking and, with the ultimate result, the *need* for drinking decreases into a faint memory.

Ornish reframes the issue from "fear of dying" to "joy of living." Participating in AA changes thoughts from "restless, irritable, and disconnected" to "happy, joyous, and free." This attitudinal shift puts change into a different context, or as Ornish says, "Joy is a more powerful motivator than fear. Telling people who are lonely and depressed that they're going to live longer if they quit smoking or change their diet and lifestyle is not motivating. Who wants to live longer when you're in chronic emotional pain?" Who wants to give up alcohol, a cherished habit? Who wants to give up the *Don't Change* Habit until something better is available?

Change is hard, difficult, painful, and often messy. Pointing your finger at others and blaming is an expression of the resistance to change. There is a book entitled *Feel the Fear and Do It Anyway* by Susan Jeffers. I love the wisdom expressed in the title. Instead of blaming others for your discomfort, you must become responsible for your own life.

> *"A friend is someone who gives you*
> *total freedom to be yourself*
> *and especially to feel, or not feel.*
> *Whatever you happen to be feeling*
> *at any moment is fine with them.*
> *That's what real love amounts to -*
> *letting a person be what he really is."*
> Jim Morrison

Instead of the monster under the bed, what you fear most, visualize yourself being happy and having the great love in your heart fully expressed to your loved ones and feel the connecting power of love when it is returned. This love-exchange is the joy Ornish refers to. Just by reading this book, you are well along the way toward changing your destructive lifestyle. The more you turn away from these habits, the more positive changes you make, the more your happiness will grow in proportion to the changes you make.

"My Life Will Change...When I Change"™

Exercise - 37

Think about your own resistance to change. How has this *Don't Change Habit* affected your life? How do you want to define your life from this point onward?

> *You might be a Chaos Person if...*
> you know you have just found
> the perfect man. The only problem seems
> to be...he comes with a warning label.

Antidote to Don't Be Real

*"Nobody can go back and start a new beginning,
but anyone can start today and make a new ending."*
Maria Robinson

The children's book *The Velveteen Rabbit* by Margery Williams has a wonderful message. In the story, the Velveteen Rabbit is a toy and is envious of the Skin Horse who is real. The Skin Horse responds to the Velveteen Rabbit's question about how he too could become real: "Real isn't how you are made. It's a thing that happens to you. It takes a long, long time."

Don't be Real is a habit we learned from our dysfunctional heritage. However, like the Velveteen Rabbit, we truly want to be real, to have the freedom of being who we are and to accept ourselves as we are. We ardently desire to take down our masks and say to the world, "This is who I am…and I am okay." This is simple…not easy.

The *Don't be Real* Habit requires you to wear an iron mask so no one can see the real you – all they see is what you present to the world. Behind the mask, your face sweats and you long to feel the cool of a summer's evening, but removing the mask means others will see you as you are, not the image you wish them to see; honest is terrifying. The antidote to change from the *Don't Be Real* Habit is simple…get real. Getting real starts with a decision to become real and then having the courage and desire to follow through with changing this destructive habit.

People break the *Don't Be Real* Habit when they get honest. They have the courage to begin to live the life they want, not one based upon what someone else wants, or live the life their parents planned for them. Being real is being true to you. Several years into my intense *Thumb Work*, someone suggested to me, "…follow my bliss." For several years, this thought echoed in my head as a faraway, foggy image, for what I wanted was to become a mental health counselor. At this time, I was working for a specialty industrial contractor. My joke was "Construction is not far from mental health." People in the construction industry chuckled at the truth revealed in this little joke.

I did not see how I could go to graduate school and work a full-time job and I plodded down the decision path worrying how I would ever pass the Graduate Record Exam (GRE) for entrance into LSU. When I took the GRE prep course, it further convinced me I was not graduate material. I thought GRE was a high barrier, maybe one impossible to overcome; graduate school was not for the likes of me.

Fortunately, life happened, and my boss laid me off from my construction job; I was immediately unemployed. This uncomfortable realization caused two hours of panic, but the calmness came when I realized I was now free. Free to pursue my bliss, I moved to Corpus Christi with the intent of getting a Master's of Science at Texas A&M University.

I still fretted about the GRE and hesitated to apply until I reread the university's entrance requirements for the third time. My fears then immediately disappeared. The GRE was not required for initial entry but only before the student completed the first nine credit hours. Once I saw this provision, I realized this allowed me to start my masters program. If I did well on my first nine hours, there was no way they would kick me out even if my GRE score were not acceptable. Free from this fear, I could follow my bliss!

When I entered the change process...recovery, my bliss was to be happy and to be able to share love in healthy ways, to do this I had to become real. How does one begin to be real? How does one become the Skin Horse? For me, I needed a group of accepting people, self-help groups, and a couple of good counselors I had learned to trust. In these environments, I discovered I could be honest, discard my mask, and begin to be real. Catholics have a safe place for honesty called confession. Although I am not Catholic, I attend a silent retreat every year where there are wonderful Jesuit Priests who help set the atmosphere for the participants to be real. Here, participants can touch base with themselves by being honest, in the quiet solitude of their own minds. This is one of the places I work on my realness.

When you wear a mask, you are not real. When you live your life based upon what others may think, you are not authentic. When you are not true to yourself and do not acknowledge your own bliss, you are not real. The more a person gets honest in an accepting environment, the more this realness becomes theirs; but unlike the Skin Horse's pronouncement, it does not "...take a long, long time." All it takes is a desire and the courage to be honest, and then doing the emotional work realness requires.

Exercise - 38

How hard is it for you to be honest? Are unexpressed secrets causing you problems? You sure about that?

What would happen if in a safe environment you told others about your deepest and darkest secrets?

You might be a Chaos Person if...
you define stress as when your brain
says "No, no, no' but what comes out
of your mouth is, "Of course, I'd be delighted."

People can literally change their brain chemistry by choosing to smile and by making the decision to be happy, as in declaring each morning… "I choose to be happy." How we think goes a long way towards how we feel. When making this choice, we can be in pain and still be happy. An interesting and wonderful phenomenon happens when we quit hiding our discomfort and share our truths and get honest with others. In this way, we can mitigate the pain and at the same time not accept the misery knocking on our door. As an unknown author so wisely said, "Pain is inevitable, misery is optional." Our realness is REAL as long as we are not hiding from our discomfort. People pay a dear price when not dealing with the powerful emotions.

However, there are times when it is not appropriate to be REAL and acknowledge the true self, and discernment is required for the time and place. Some people are not safe with the intimacy we need to share; people who are judgmental, gossips and those who do not listen and want to "fix" our problems are not safe people.

A good example of this occurs when people who are not REAL, smile when they are in pain. This smile conveys a false message; it is a mask. In therapy, I often experience clients seeking to avoid the pain of their current reality by smiling. As gently as possible, I challenge them to take off their smiley mask and be REAL. When people smile to avoid the emotional pain, smiling keeps them stuck. It has a novocaine effect, keeping them from the discomfort and ultimately the healing available when they work through the pain. Smiling to hide from the truth then becomes a false statement, a place to hide their true selves and not be REAL.

> *"...we all live our lives in chains,*
> *and we never even know*
> *we have the key."*
> the Eagles -Already Gone

Give yourself permission to grieve when hurt. Give yourself permission to have whatever feelings you now have. Give yourself permission to confront the loss and work through the pain. Not being REAL is a way of hiding from this unpleasant reality and interferes with the healing process.

Another manifestation of the *Don't Be Real* Habit is a person who "has to be right." My friend and counselor, Andy Shurr, asked me, "What is the largest addiction in the world?" Before I could answer, he said, "Looking good and being right."

You can especially see this dynamic in religion and politics. These topics have a tremendous potential for conflict; rigid thinking about these two polarizing topics has caused many wars. A friend of mine and I had a discussion concerning our views of the spiritual realm. Here we really agreed with each other; we were on the same page, connected. During the same conversation, we then drifted into the political arena where we held opposing views on the same subject. I could feel a wall going up between my friend and me, where I judged him, found him "wrong", and then rejected him. I started arguing with him, and upon later reflection, I realized in this discussion I felt I had to be right, and it was my responsibility to show him the error of his ways. This hard attitude of mine created separation between us.

In the comic strip, Hagar the Horrible, Hagar and his whimsical side-kick, Lucky Eddie, were once involved in a big battle with the enemy. Lucky Eddie asks, "Why are we fighting so hard?" and Hagar emphatically responds, "Because we're right!" The sidekick looks at him and inquires, "The other side is fighting so hard because…they are wrong?"

The attitude of being right creates black and white thinking: "Either you are for me or against me" or "It's my way or the highway." With rigid positions, there is no room for gray. Black and white thinking limits understanding and feedback, two necessary ingredients for successful resolution in creative conflict and successful understanding.

Exercise – 39

Does your thinking have the sharpness of black and white? What would you have to let go of in order to lose your absolutism, your cherished rigidity, how you view life in black and white terms, and enter the peaceful gray between your extremes?

You might be a Chaos Person if...
you never put off till tomorrow
what you can put off till next week.

People who rid themselves of the *Don't Be Real* habit discover a wonderful world of living authentic lives, being really alive where their insides match their outsides. They do not have a false front or worry what others may think. They are true to themselves; they are authentic. This creates an element of trust; people trust REAL people. Once people are REAL, they become trustworthy. People who are not REAL are uncertainties and do not yet warrant trust.

When REAL people make promises to themselves and others, they work hard on living up to their commitments. REAL people do not have to lie, exaggerate, or brag for they are self-contained in self-understanding and acceptance of themselves. REAL people can make a mistake knowing that even when they do, it is only a mistake and just because the outcome was not to their liking, they know…THEY are not a mistake. REAL have the attitude *this is who I am…and I am good enough, right now…just as I am*. People who have chosen REAL have already clicked their heels together and returned home.

> *"To be fully seen by somebody,*
> *and be loved anyhow-*
> *this is a human offering that can*
> *border on miraculous."*
> Elizabeth Gilbert

Exercise -40

Are you good enough…now? If your answer is not positive, write about your definition of yourself and what you would really like to believe about yourself. What would it take for you to get to your goal?

You might be a Chaos Person if…
you eat a mouth full of Oreos Cookies
before having your teeth cleaned.

Antidote to Don't Respect Boundaries

"The moment that judgment stops
through acceptance of what is,
you are free of the mind.
You have made room for
love, for joy, for peace."
Eckart Tolle

What separates one person from another are boundaries. The more severe the dysfunction you experienced growing up, the more difficult boundaries are for you. Children from a dysfunctional family either do not know how or are unwilling to set boundaries, and/or they violate others' limits, unwilling to draw their own lines in the sand, while also violating others' lines.

A client of mine had a disconcerting habit of raising her voice when excited. Adding to this, she would point her finger at you for added emphasis. This lack of respect of personal boundaries caused others not to want to listen to her, and she was often misunderstood. When she felt this disconnection, her strong emotions kicked in and she took this lack of understanding personally; she did not feel respected. Not having another coping skill, she did what many do when experiencing rejection; she raised her voice, so much that other people thought she was yelling at them. Her behaviors and other's reaction caused this cycle of disrespect to escalate and was a source of irritation to everyone. It threatened her career.

This client was a naturally an enthusiastic person who wanted to be successful at work and had many skills valued by her employer. How she communicated limited her effectiveness, causing her to doubt herself, and to think about changing jobs. I equated her unabashed enthusiasm as "Muddy Paws." She looked at me uncertain of my meaning. "Muddy Paws?" she echoed. "Yes," I replied, "you are like a playful puppy who wants your attention so badly she jumps up on you with her muddy paws, violating your space and soiling your clothes.

"Sometimes you just have to
regret things and move on."
Charlaine Harris

Exercise -41

Ever had a dog jump on you with muddy paws? What is your reaction to this dog? Have you ever known a person with "muddy paws"? What is your reaction to someone who is hyper-excitable, boundary violating, excessively verbal, or demanding of their own way? How muddy are your paws?

You might be a Chaos Person if...
you know quiet meditation would probably help,
if only you could sit still long enough.

Have you ever received an email or text with the message all in caps? These messages are often vexing to read and appear to be packed with emotions. When reading this type of message it feels as though the sender is screaming at us. My client's method of expressing herself was like receiving a text message all in caps, and anyone listening to this enthusiastic person felt her lack of respect and did not want to give her the understanding she so desperately sought, thereby compounding the isolation she felt.

In my most dysfunctional state, my *muddy paws* came out as attention-grabbing humor. I had to have the focus on me, since I was the *Family Mascot.* I brought my abandonment needs into everyday interactions, such as the classrooms, social situations, and even at work. I had to have the spotlight, and with this demand, I could be and often was disruptive with my humor.

To begin to change, a person has to know his own boundaries and be prepared to defend those limits. Being able to say, "No," is a necessary ingredient in a healthy lifestyle. Do you sometimes say "Yes" when you really mean "No"? In this case, you are not being true to yourself and are discounting your own boundaries. Someone once said, "If you are more than fair to another, then you are being less than fair to yourself."

The truth is, we tend to train people how we want to be treated. If others know that you have wishy-washy boundaries and they are free to walk all over you; the result is…you become a doormat. We have actually trained others to do this when we allow people to wipe their muddy feet on us. After all, we are doormats.

In the Kingwood, Texas Al-Anon clubhouse where I spent many hours doing *Thumb Work*, I looked on the wall one night and saw a woven mat with a beautiful multi-colored butterfly in the center of the dark fibers. When it came my time to share, I remarked about this wall hanging: "See that beautiful butterfly on the mat hanging on the wall?" I asked. "I think it symbolizes what I'm attempting to do. Before recovery, I was a doormat where I allowed others to clean their boots on me. My butterfly became covered in dirt. What I want to do now is pick up my doormat, clean off the years of accumulated dirt and grime, and instead of leaving it on the floor again for others to soil, I want to mount it on the wall for all to enjoy." Many heads nodded in agreement. From this realization, I now do not leave my doormat on the floor allowing others to walk on it. It is much more difficult for others to wipe their feet on my doormat since it is now hanging on the wall.

I had a roommate, John Williams, who wrote thought-provoking songs. He wrote one about me, *Everyone Needs a Clown in Their Life*. It is a real treat to have someone write a song about you! One of my favorites of John's songs is entitled *Wickie-Woo*. You should thank your lucky stars you are reading this and not hearing my singing. Several lines I especially like are "Turn around and it might be you, making you sad, what is making you blue…*Wickie-Woo*." The best line of the song, tying into the doormat theme is, "…get yourself off of the floor and I won't have to step on you… *Wickie-Woo*."

Exercise - 42

What do you see when you look into the mirror? Do you see a confident person? Do you see someone who can easily be run-over? What would it take for you to change what you see in the mirror? Can you take your doormat, shake it out, wash it off, and hang it on the wall instead of leaving it on the floor for others to step upon. How difficult would it be for you to adopt the mindset of...*doormat no more*?

You might be a Chaos Person if...
when the going gets tough...
you wet your pants.

What I hope you are able to see in your mirror is an image of you as an assertive person. In this vision, you decided to remove your doormat, the same doormat people walked over for so long, and now you are saying "No." Nobody can step on your doormat without your permission for it is no longer on the floor...*Wickie Woo*. The image you see in the mirror is YOU with your doormat safely hanging on the wall awaiting admiration. The image is YOU, teaching others how YOU want to be treated. Doormat no more!...*Wickie Woo*.

As you look at your doormat, picture your likeness weaved into the center; it is a beautiful design called you. Following the *Wickie-Woo* advice, pick up your beautiful doormat all soiled by many feet, then scrub it cleaning of the years of encrusted mud from the many feet treading upon it. Now, you have a choice. You can hang it on the wall for people to appreciate its beauty, or you can leave it on the floor where it always has been for people to walk on. Your doormat... your choice... wall hanging... or... doormat? Why are we doormats always so surprised when others wipe their feet on us?

Exercise - 43

Take a picture of yourself saying "No." Have your hands out, palms away from you and your palms pointed upward. Keep this photo handy as a reminder of how powerful this image is, and how it can work for you.

You might be a Chaos Person if...
you apologize so often,
you have to apologize
for apologizing so often.

Lagniappe for Parents

("*Lagniappe*" is Cajun for something given freely and for good measure.)

Children see structure as love! When a family does not have good boundaries, does not follow through, and/or does not consistently enforce family rules, children are not in an environment to thrive and they do not feel loved. When there is good structure (not rigidity), where good boundaries are coupled with respect, and understanding, children thrive and feel safe. You may not have received this loving structure when you were raised, that is unfortunate. The key question you now get to ask yourself: "What structure do my children need that they are not getting now?

You might be a Chaos Person if...
you heard that "two wrongs
don't make a right"
so you tried for three.

Antidote to Don't Accept

"My happiness grows in direct proportion to my acceptance,
and inverse proportion to my expectations."
Michael J. Fox

W hat separates human beings? Is it geography, race, ideology, religion, or politics? All of these things have been the source of conflicts ever since Cain slew Abel. Putting labels on others creates a black hole of disregard where judgment thrives and schisms deepen. The slave and the slave owner are victims of the same system. I cannot enslave you without being there to be your overseer. By the same reasoning, I cannot call you a "jerk" without viewing all our interactions thereafter filtered through this "jerk" label I inflicted upon you, and then searching for evidence to justify the correctness of the title I gave you.

Is there an antidote? Yes, acceptance.

Acceptance is the most beautiful word in any language; this beautiful concept can only exist when you allow other people to be who they are and do not imprison them with your definition of what is right, proper, correct, or some other limiting criteria. Decreasing the black and white in your thinking allows for an expansive area of gray, allowing you to live your life and me to live mine. Acceptance sets us all free! This simple change of thought creates a wonderful space for happiness to thrive.

When I first started studying acceptance, I was rather judgmental. I was sure my beliefs, thoughts, and worldview were fundamentally correct and unshakeable. Others who were not conforming were devalued; they just were not as smart as me, right? Back then, I was black and white; you are for me or against me – you are good or bad – you agreed with me or you were an idiot. You either went to the same church as me or you did not understand what was correct; you either agreed with my political views or you were totally uninformed. If you rooted for my team, you were okay, but if not, you were the enemy. This attitude made me an island where only a few people were allowed and then only when acquiescing to my superior intellect, magnificent wisdom, omniscient aura; all covering an incredibly low self-esteem. When you did not conform to my definitions, you were expelled from my island. My isolation became darker and lonelier; but "I know I'm right!" I shouted this theme again and again into the ever-increasing darkness as my loneliness covered me like a cold and wet blanket and I withdrew deeper and deeper into my unhappiness.

This pattern of thought ignored the wonderful world of a huge unexplored gray area existing between the polar opposites. Rigid positions create extremes, especially in politics and religion. Having one religion held in a higher standard than others is condemning others and judging them as "not okay." This attitude is what causes the majority to persecute the minority because of perceived or real differences; since you are not like me, you must not be okay. Since I have my majority position to justify my beliefs, I am right and you are wrong.

When my isolation was complete, my darkest of days, when it was either reach out or die, I finally reached out and found a different way of living. I discovered one of the root causes of my unhappiness was my habit of thinking in absolute terms. When I held an absolute position about anything, I would put a handy label on it so I could judge whether it was good or bad, right or wrong, for me or against me, my way or the highway. This was how I navigated through life. Some of these labels were racial, sexual, political, or gender judgment; I would not tolerate differences! With these labels so necessary to maintain my rigid thinking, it was easy to categorize others and have a convenient method of judging and then rejecting them. The more judgmental a person is the sadder they are.

I regret those harsh attitudes and now exist in a wonderful world of "live and let live." When I learned about the gray space between the black and white of absolute terms, I began to experience more peace. The more I expanded my gray areas, the more peace I experienced in my life.

When I finally recognized my lack of acceptance, at the height of my own arrogance and perfected dysfunction, the pain was overwhelming; I knew I had to change. If peacefulness and acceptance was going to be mine, I had to do two things differently. The first thing was to get off my judge's bench, take off my heavy black robe, lay down my judgment gavel, and cease looking down at others from my lofty judge's position-three feet above contradiction. I had to discard my arrogance and get on the same level as others. Being on the same level, I could now look others in the eye and allow them to be who they were, which allowed me to be me. Twelve Step Programs call this acceptance, as in "Live and Let Live."

The second concern required to live in the gray is breaking the *Don't Respect Boundaries* habit, as discussed in an earlier section. I have to know where you stop and I begin. I have to respect other people's boundaries and defend them as strongly as I defend my own. After identifying my personal boundaries, I need to know how to defend them effectively with methods that do not add to the problem.

How would you like all your problems solved today? All your problems solved in one sentence? Is this a tall tale, propaganda, political sound bites line, or religious dogma? Have I lost it? Maybe? Read on.

In the *Big Book of Alcoholics Anonymous*, there is a wonderful paragraph on acceptance. I marvel at its simple but powerful wisdom and then relax into the quiet comfort this attitude has on my life:

> "And acceptance is the answer to all my problems
> today. When I am disturbed, it is because I find
> some person, place, thing, or situation-some fact of
> my life-unacceptable to me, and I can find no seren-
> ity until I accept that person, place, thing, or situa-
> tion as being exactly the way it is supposed o be at
> this moment…unless I accept life completely on
> life's terms, I cannot be happy. I need to concentrate
> not so much on what needs to be changed in the
> world as what needs to be changed in me and in my
> attitudes." *Alcoholics Anonymous*
>
> *And acceptance is the answer to all my problems…"*

Wow, does this mean, all I have to do to solve all my problems to-day is to accept them? Exactly …the answer couldn't be that, it's too simple, right? Acceptance will solve your entire discontent-ment, for indeed in acceptance, what you now face is reality. What causes you discomfort is what you are unwilling to accept, the re-ality as it is at this moment "…living life on life's terms."

In acceptance, you are not bemoaning your unhappiness and magi-cally wishing things were different. In acceptance, you are not the victim exclaiming to anyone who will listen about how unfair life is. In acceptance, you decide to accept "…life on life's terms." You may not like the reality or the "…person, place, thing, or situa-tion…" facing you now, but the "person, place, or situation" is the reality you have to face at this moment…*Wickie Woo*

Can you change the reality of this moment? No, of course not. Can you accept the "…person, place, thing, or situation…" as being ex-actly the way it is …at this moment? If you want to be happy, separating the two is the key. My friend, John Williams, wrote another song with the refrain of "…when reality hits, it's not always what you want it to be." Reality may not be what you want it to be, but it is the reality you now must face. You can deny this reality and try to wish it away, or you can accept it and not waste any energy on wanting it to be different.

Acceptance does not mean you cannot work for positive change, but it does mean you have accepted the reality of life as it is cur-rently happening. With this realization, you do not have to waste precious moments of living whining about how unfair life is. It means in acceptance… I can be happy.

This year on Gay Pride Day, Nathan Ryan the Assistant Minister of the Unitarian Church quoted the Pastor, Steve Crump, in his sermon. In 1984, Crump said to his congregation, "I feel I am called to affirm the expression of love of consenting adults, whether that means a man and a woman, or between two men or two women."

Had I been in this audience in 1984 and heard this statement, I would have cringed, been repulsed, and stood up and walked out in a rage. For back then my judgmental mind was rampant, I did not accept others in the spirit of *live and let live*, and I was very homo-phobic. I felt a profound sense of release when I realized I no longer judged others by what I did not understand, or what was different from me. When I was homophobic, in my righteous judgment, I was separated, distant from myself and thus was distant from others.

My graduation ceremony from my homophobia was a day in 1989 when I decided it was time to get rid of my self-imposed separation from a group I did not understand and formally hated. I decided if I could give a gay man a hug, I would finally be free. Fortunately, at that time, I had met Ted, a man who I had already learned to respect despite his declared sexual attraction for men. Ted and I attended the same Twelve Step Program where we got to know each other in the honest environment this program creates. After one meeting in front of the lingering and chatting fellowship, I walked up to Ted and <u>said</u>, "Can I give you a hug?" Hugs are a part of the traditions found in the Twelve Steps Programs and in this environment, participants hug one another and it's okay for a man to hug another man. He said, "Sure." The hug was warm, connecting, but non-sexual; it was a good feeling. After he hugged me, I was instantaneously free from the crushing weight of my homophobia. I now began living in acceptance. Many years later, I told him how important his hug had been to me.

Acceptance still gives me problems for there are times when someone or some group kicks in my...*I'm better than you* arrogance and I must really struggle to accept them. The strange and wondrous part of this discovery is: I cannot reject another without rejecting me, however the more I practice acceptance the more I can accept myself.

After those years of judging others, I have since learned that we are all connected through this universal tapestry called life. If I view others as separate, different, and do not include them because they are not like me, I miss so much of what there is to know, I miss a profound connection with another, and my peace is severely limited.

You might be a Chaos Person if...
you are so tactful at work
when firing someone afterwards
they then invite you to lunch.

Exercise - 44

Write about your lack of acceptance and what it has cost you. Do you put labels on other groups and look down at them with disdain? Where are you lacking acceptance?

Can your wasted energy be more productive if you accept the reality of what is, stop judging others, and live the gray? Do you spend psychic energy being the victim? What will happen once you accept this "...person, place, thing, or situation..." as being exactly the way it is?

"Lead us from unreal to real,
from lethargy to light,
from fear of death
to oneness with the eternal."
Hindu chant

Can you turn your wishing it were different into some positive action to change this "…person, place, thing, or situation? What will you do differently?

Do your best to live your life in acceptance. Be aware when your acceptance slips and you revert to judgment with black and white thinking. Pick out someone who has a different point of view than you: maybe a different religion, political party, or life style. Practice listening to them with acceptance; not necessarily agreeing with them but trying hard to understand them. Write down what happened and how you felt when doing the experiment.

You might be in the Chaos Habit if…
you are so worried about dying
you forget to live.

Universal Cure

What do you want when you really need to talk? Do you want undivided attention, understanding, and acceptance? Sure. If you are lucky enough to receive the gift of listening, can it be later ruined by judgment? When you are sharing what is heavy on your soul do you need anyone to "fix" your problem? Do you want him or her to attempt to take control of your life with their unsolicited wisdom and insist on you living your life as they deem appropriate? Or would you like him or her to understand you are quite capable of solving your problems?

When one person attempts to "fix it" for the other person, the connection of acceptance is snapped and the sender and receiver miss an opportunity for understanding. When someone uses statements such as "should" or "should not", it is an attempt at control. When you judge another using controlling words, you are not a good companion or listener; you are sitting in judgment and not listening with acceptance.

You do not have to agree that the other person is right, but as an Active Listener, you must agree that others have the right to be understood! These "should statements" also come in the form of *ought/ought not, must/must not*, and sometimes not using the actual words but expressing a commanding should-type statement. At one time, my kids sometimes called me *Daddy Should-Ought*. Now, when my kids or grandkids come to me with their problems, I consider it a sacred honor I must not abuse with SHOULDs. Despite this effort, honesty especially with someone you love, is incredibly hard.

What I discovered works much better than SHOULDs is helping others develop options. When I'm asked, I assist people who seek my counsel to develop choices. The first question I ask them once the problem is defined: "What are your options?" If they do not know ...I do not offer my "wisdom" but instead help to explore their world for their (not mine) possible options. If they are still stuck, I ask if I could present a few options from my point of view. If my suggestions are what they want, I continue; if not...I do not inflict my ideas upon them.

After I'd learned this wonderful coping skill, my son asked my advice. I helped him develop three or four options. Then I helped him with the pros and cons of each option. I knew what I thought best but these were his choices for his life...not mine. After he developed a set of options and ran through the pros and cons of each, I had to laugh when he reverted to our old dysfunctional pattern and asked, "Okay, Dad, what should I do?"

I responded, "Well you got option one, option two, and option three. Which one are you going to chose?"

"No, Dad, what should I do?"

I again responded, "Well, you got this option, and this option, and the other option is this...Which one are you going to choose?"

"Dad, you've been telling me what to do for 18 years...What should I do?"

"Well, son, as I see it, you've got option one, option two, and the third other option is this."

In this exchange, I successfully resisted the almost overwhelming temptation to give my son a SHOULD. I had to let him go into the world to make his own decisions, his own mistakes, and trust that he would find his own happiness. I had to let go of worry and transform the wasted energy of worrying into the power of belief...as what I told him: "I believe in you." I do not remember what question my son was struggling with then nor do I remember what my son chose. I know this exercise worked out well, and this interaction became a pattern for many father-son discussions we had and continue to have. Recently I called him with a problem I was having and he helped me using this same method; helping me develop my own options.

Parents need their children to fail. (Wow! What a horrific statement!) Would it not be better if they fell short when they are still with you and you are still available to help them pick up the pieces from their failures? Remember, how you learned to ride a bicycle...exactly, by falling off. If we do not let them fall down, they will take forever to learn to ride. If we do not let go of the seat, how can they ever be on their own? When we witness their lack of success, it is so easy to reinforce the SHOULD we previously gave them with a judgmental statement…"See, I told you so." Instead, when others face failure, try this wonderful question: "What did you learn?"

We men are especially bad about this. Men do three things very well. We build things; we fix things; and we blow things up! When we love someone, our natural instinct is to fix his or her problems. After all, this is what men do best and often this desire is our best attempt to show love. Men, this may hurt your ego but… your loved ones do not need to be fixed. What they really need is for you to listen to them, to give them your understanding, and your help in working through their options. Most of all they need your belief that they can effectively solve their own problems. They will feel more love from you if you extend this attitude than if you revert to your natural position of *Mister Fixer* or *Daddy Should-Ought.*

Now, there is a place for SHOULD statements, such as "You should be at work at 8:00 AM, or "You should get this order to the customer quicker," or "You should look both ways before you cross the street." These are the appropriate places for SHOULD statements. It is better if parents, bosses, coworkers, and significant others are aware of when to use a SHOULD statement and when not to. As you can see, demand statements are an attempt to control another. Ultimately, demand statements are counterproductive and cause conflict and self-doubt.

When my twenty-year marriage ended, my daddy called and told me, "David, this is what you *should* do. You call her and get down on bended knee and beg her forgiveness."

After I hung up the phone, I was in a two-day depression until I figured out what had happened. My father, who I respected more than anyone in the world, just told me I was not okay because I was not living my life based upon what he thought I needed to do. He gave me a SHOULD. In his effort to show love to his son, he inadvertently put me in a depression.

The next time I was with him, I said, "Dad, telling me what I *should or should not* do is not what I need from you. What I need is understanding and acceptance. I do not need you telling me what to do or not to do."

He immediately understood what I was telling him…"thank you, Dad." For the rest of his life, he did his best to give me what I needed from him, understanding and acceptance instead of a SHOULD statement. Sometimes he would preface his comments by, "David, this is not a SHOULD, but…"

Sometimes they were actual SHOULD statements but his acknowledging made all the difference in the world. Remember, SHOULD statements come in the form of *should, should not, must or must not*, and sometimes people don't use these actual words but the message is clear when translated…it is an order.

Albert Ellis, the famous psychologist, has a wonderful way of conveying this message in a way you will never forget. When you tell someone, what he or she *should* do…know what you are doing?

> *You are SHOULDING on them.*
> *Uck, you just SHOULD on me.*
> *So, do not SHOULD on people!*

Okay, now with this new awareness you are not going to SHOULD on people. What do you do when someone you care about has a problem and you know the answer? You care about this person, but with this new awareness, you do not want to SHOULD on them. This poses a double blind…you care and want to help but do not want to control, so what do you do?

Instead of giving them a SHOULD, you can ask them… "I have some experience that may benefit, do you want to hear it?" If they say "no," just shut up, validating their right to say no. But human nature being what it is, their curiosity usually will overcome any resistance and they will later come back to you…on their terms. This is how we show respect to others.

Exercise – 45

Study this word SHOULD in three different situations

- Observe other people trying to control others with SHOULD statements.

- Identify what you feel when someone gives you an inappropriate SHOULD.

- Then the biggest SHOULD of them all. The SHOULDs you give yourself.

Exercise - 46

The next three questions may seem rhetorical, but unless asked and answered we may miss an important message.

- Are you accepting of yourself when you beat yourself up with the SHOULDS?

- Is this behavior working for you or do you need something else?

- What do you plan to do differently?

Continue your SHOULD work by finishing this form.

In the first column, write a SHOULD you typically give yourself. In the second column, rewrite the SHOULD so it is not a SHOULD. I provided several examples to get you started.

Original SHOULD	Revised Statement
I should eat healthier food.	I choose to eat healthier foods.
I should have gotten the promotion.	It would have been great if I got the promotion. I did not and now I have to figure out if I am going to stay and keep on improving or leave the company.

Absolute statements, especially those of the SHOULD variety, transmit messages we may not want to express. Vow to yourself, "I will be more aware of absolute statements. In significant relationships, I will NEVER use the words 'Always' and 'Never' again"— unless of course you want to start a fight and if this is the case just acknowledge your desire and have a good one!

> *You might be a Chaos Person if...*
> you're so overprotective of your kid,
> you installed a seatbelt on his Big Wheel.

Antidotes Summary

To sum up the antidotes, consider an illustration about John, an alcoholic. Using an extreme illustration often makes it easier to understand the principles. In this example, John now attends Alcoholics Anonymous meetings after many years of drinking. What is he doing differently? He understands *all* of the dysfunctional family habits, and you will see him break the dysfunctional habits learned in his youth as he chooses to do the opposite of his early learning!

Although this example is about how John used AA to change his life around, other people have found different methods of overcoming these habits with the help of self-help programs like Al-Anon, Overeaters Anonymous, Narcotics Anonymous, Gambling Anonymous, and Codependent Anonymous. Others have found success in therapy, and still others after obtaining a different perspective on life by talking to trusted friends or clergy.

Before AA, John hid in the shame of his addiction, self-loathing, and misery. He drank excessively to hide from past failures, bad memories, and disturbing thoughts. Not wanting to feel painful feelings, he used alcohol to self-medicate his emotions. With the role models of other participants he learned it is okay to be honest and now he openly talks with other AA members, his sponsor, and recovery friends. John broke the *Don't Talk* Habit.

When he first walked through the doors of AA, he hoped this group could help relieve his suffering. After experiencing this fellowship with others who were also suffering from addiction, he began to trust. Here was an organization he realized could help him and all he had to do was show up and participate. It took a lot of courage, but John was able to talk in the meetings and trust that other participants would both understand and not be judgmental. John broke the *Don't Trust* Habit.

When John first attended AA, he buried his emotions under his addiction, but through the recovery process he began to feel. He became emotionally available. His feelings returned. He no longer felt he had to run away or hide from the pain, and he realized he did not have to medicate himself to escape from the strong emotions pulsating through him. He realized how he could use his emotions to navigate through life, instead of hiding from his feelings. When John began using the Mood Chart, he broke the *Don't Feel* Habit.

During AA meetings, anyone who has a desire to quit drinking can take a Desire Chip. At his very first meeting, John picked up a plastic Desire Chip signifying to himself and others his yearning for a better way of living. It did not mean he immediately gave up drinking alcohol, but just his wish to change. Before AA, John would never acknowledge to anyone, let alone a group of strange people, that he had any problems. Now at most AA meetings, John shares with the group what is going on with him. He talks with his sponsor, and just by his attendance he puts himself in a place of change. John broke the *Don't Change* Habit. He sees now a purpose and a meaning in life, he is experiencing acceptance and understanding, and he can now express and receive love in much healthier ways.

The only requirement for success in the change process is honesty. John became honest and shared his darkest secrets with others who listened to him, accepted him as he was, and did not judge him, thus allowing John to begin the arduous process of becoming real. John broke the *Don't Be Real* Habit.

Hearing the stories from other participants about how their behavior hurt the people they loved, John realized how much pain he too had inflicted on others - and himself. His behavior limited the love available to him from those he cared about most, and restricted the love he was able to express. He then recognized other people's boundaries and discovered he also needed to set limits of acceptable behavior. John got honest in the meetings and discovered he was not a demon but a wounded person who had some coping skills that did not work; he had some learned habits interfering with his happiness. Before recovery, lies or omissions were his way of protecting his abandonment fears. He now tells the truth. John broke the *Don't Be Honest* Habit.

When John put himself in the company of others who also suffered from dysfunctional lifestyles, he was amazed at the acceptance he received from the group. They listened to him, doing their best to understand and relate to what he was saying, and all this without judging him. In this loving, supportive environment, John learned he could accept others as they were and not try to change them. He learned to live life on life's terms. Amazingly, this acceptance paved the way toward his self-forgiveness. John broke the *Don't Accept* Habit.

You may not be an alcoholic like John, but if you search for places of healing and acceptance such as those mentioned at the beginning of this section, you will find what you are looking for. Like John, you too can break any or all of the dysfunctional family habits you've acquired. I believe in you.

In one word, I can sum up my experiences when I lived by the code of the dysfunctional family habits...*disconnection.* Most of the world's problems stem from the feeling of disconnection, left out, not included, and different, all metastasized into the certainty of not being loved. With this feeling of disconnection, you try to fill this hole in your soul with other things - such as alcohol, drugs, gambling, workaholic, perfectionism, compulsive religious fervor, enmeshing your lives with others - all in an attempt to stave off experiencing this internal void, dark pit of the human soul. Ultimately, all will fail. However when you feel connected to yourself, the lonesome valley you have to walk is not so dark, fearful, or anxiety provoking; instead it becomes calm waters, blue skies, and springtime flowers.

In 2001, my longtime friend, Blair Stocker, died and I returned to Lake Charles, LA for the funeral services. I lived in Lake Charles for twelve years and Blair was one of the many friends I had during those days. There was always something special about Blair; I felt I could connect with him if I ever needed to, but my denial of my issues was so great I never did. Back then I did not know how to ask for help. I did not know how to be honest and I missed the comfort my friend could offer.

The services were held in the First Presbyterian Church where I used to attend and, even after 20 years, when I walked into the sanctuary, it had not changed at all. Many of the people I knew back then were in attendance, and they even invited the old preacher out of retirement; so the stage was set in very familiar surroundings.

There was my friend, Blair, in the casket at the front of the church and I was sitting in a padded pew. Sadness suddenly struck me, like getting punched hard in the stomach, and I unashamedly wept. However, my tears were not for Blair or his family; he was in a far better place.

My sadness was for me, remembering myself sitting in these same pews Sunday after Sunday, doing everything my culture, family, religion, and work ethic told me to do to be happy. I had a beautiful wife, two young children, and an important and well-paying job. I was a Cub Scout master, an elder in the Presbyterian Church, and a Little League coach. I did all these things I thought would bring me peace and happiness...all failed. I felt completely disconnected. Looking back, I could feel how utterly miserable I had been. Back then, I did not know why I was so miserable, but my tears were now of joy. At this service, I was not miserable...I did not feel the disconnection I experienced 20 years ago. I now felt connected.

My connection journey began when I started doing *Thumb Work*, learning how to be honest, to find and to use coping skills that expressed love instead of hurt and pain. I did this by putting myself in places of healing and finally learning how to love myself again. My disconnection from the world started with my disconnection from myself. The more I regained the inner connection, the easier I could then connect to others, and then to my world. Once connected, I did not have to judge others or myself; I could be free to be who I was and allow others to be who they really are. When connected to the world, I could see the beauty in others and accept them as they really are, beautiful, magnificent, and free.

My friend, Tom Lusk, made a wonderful statement about this phenomenon when he said, "And wouldn't there be heaven on earth when all humans learn self-love." Yes, Tom, when we are connected to ourselves with healthy self-love, we contribute toward that day when we will have heaven on earth. I had to journey through a lot of pain during my self-discovery journey, and sitting in that pew at Blair's service I was so glad I made the trip from disconnection to connection, from self-loathing to self-love. The tears of joy I experienced were the celebration of this journey.

> *"To be rooted is perhaps the most important and least recognized need of the human soul."*
> Simone Weil

It would be a chaotic trip indeed if you started out for a destination and did not know where you were going. Having a goal is necessary for a road trip, and it is equally important when beginning the self-change process. Having a destination is a wonderful guiding point for accomplishing what you set out to achieve.

Exercise - 47

In this exercise, write a Declaration Statement of how you want to live your life. Put a lot of detail in it, not thinking of where you are now, but knowing that by doing *Thumb Work*, you can accomplish the loftiest of goals. As an example, my Declaration Statement is found in the Appendix, and you may use any part of it you wish.

I wrote my goals on December 8, 1988 in the form of a Declaration Statement when I was still struggling with a lot of dysfunction in my life. Like you, I wanted to change. On a cold day in December, I followed my bliss and took a risk; I wrote about what I wanted. When I wrote my statement, I had many doubts about achieving these lofty goals. As I reread that statement, written so many years ago in the midst of my misery and pain, it has all come true for me. When you declare what you intend and do the necessary *Thumb Work*, it will come true for you as well. I believe you were created to be magnificent and by declaring your intent to live up to the promise you inherited at birth, your goals will come true.

> *"I've always believe that anything you vividly imagine, ardently desire, sincerely believe, and enthusiastically act upon, must, absolutely must come to pass."*
> Skip Bertman, Coach
> LSU National Baseball Champions 1991, 93, 96, 97, 2000

Part VI – Relapse

*"Once you've seen a solution to the disease
that's tearing you apart,
relapsing is never fun."*
Anthony Kiedis

Do you remember the example in the Introduction about the bicycle you learned to ride by falling? You are now on your change journey and I wish you well but also I hope you fail. I hope you fail for good reason. I also hope after each time you fall you will pick yourself up off the dusty street and climb back on the recovery bicycle.

My tennis coach gives me new instructions about how to make a certain shot. After he explains it, he demonstrates it several times. Now, it is my turn to try. Learning a new shot is difficult, for I want to continue to do it my old way. I have not yet developed the muscle memory of perfecting the shot. Even with the picture of his perfect form and the coach's excellent description, I have to experience the shot on my own and receive additional coaching after each attempt. I have yet to master the game of tennis, as my teammates will readily attest, but if I do not learn from a coach, I will continue the same patterns as before.

I see others who do not take lessons, but because of their natural athleticism some are good tennis players. I also see many who get better and better at their same old style, never taking the time or energy to examine how they are hitting. They get better at doing the shot in their old dysfunctional method; the results are limited in improving their game.

Give yourself permission to fail. You are not perfect and it is okay not to be perfect. Each time you find yourself in the same dysfunctional patterns you do not want to repeat, you have the opportunity to use the failure as a learning experience. Be your own coach and ask yourself, "How I can do this differently next time?"

American culture teaches us to work hard, strive for perfection, and when not perfect, to be hard on ourselves. Self-kindness is contrary to what we learned as a child at our parent's knee. Working hard to achieve goals is a good quality we all need to emulate. The problem arises when these goals, dreams, and aspirations are not being achieved. When we miss the magical plateau of perfection, we tend to beat ourselves up. Is this you?

When we attempt to change from chaos to peace, we will make mistakes. When this happens, because of our perfectionism, we get down on ourselves. Does it really help to abuse ourselves? If we abuse ourselves, will better results follow?

We learned from our caregivers that if we extended love, kindness, and acceptance to ourselves…well, we just might get the "big-head" and what would the neighbors say? From this teaching, we learned to bash ourselves, find fault, criticize, and judge ourselves harshly.

Do you have a Self-Whip? Do you beat yourself up with this whip? Would you like to stop beating yourself up with the whip of self-condemnation? If you are ready to get rid of the horrible whip, hold your hand out and visualize your Self-Whip in great detail. Now put it down in a corner of your room. Here you will always know where to pick it up again to self-flagellate. Most people think that once they throw away their whip they will never want to retrieve it; oh, how I wish it were so. When a client gives up their self-whip, meaning they earnestly want to stop beating themselves up, I pretend I am putting it on top of the many other whips clients have given me over the years. When they give me their whip, I always tell them as I store it on top of the pile, "You know where this whip is and any time you wish it back you can either ask for it or just squeeze under my door and fish yours out." This is a ridiculous illustration, but it is so instructive, for it is your whip and only you can decide how to handle your self-abuse. Do you want to get rid of your whip? Or do you want to keep it? Once given away, do you want to retrieve it? Okay so you want to give yours away… then say aloud, "I now let my whip go."

After you let go of your Self-Whip, you may again later feel the need to self-trash yourself. When that happens, declare your need to thrash yourself again and let the floggings begin; go ahead beat yourself up. Never fear, if this desire arises, you know exactly where to find your whip…just where you left it; remember…you may retrieve it any time you wish.

I did this exercise with one client. After turning over his self-whip to me for safekeeping, he later felt the need for self-abuse. He then told me, "Give me my whip back." I pretended to return it and he used it to hurt himself again. When finished, he returned it to my imaginary-but-real Self-Whip pile in the corner of my office. You are like this client…you are in control. You can self-flagellate at any time, or you can be gentle on yourself.

What would happen if you put away the Self-Whip and started extending love to yourself? What would happen if you talked to yourself as you would to a loved one? What would happen if you decided to fall in love with yourselves? Instead of condemning yourself, what would happen if you worked on understanding and accepting your reality? You are not perfect. You make mistakes, but just because you make a mistake, it does not mean you ARE a mistake. This does not mean you cannot strive for excellence. However, it means the state of perfection is an elusive goal; demanding something so obscure as almost unattainable and can become a compulsive, crazy making squirrel-on-a-wheel way of living. Having goals, desires, and dreams is healthy but if you allow these wonderful goals to become your master, the Self-Whip comes out when you experience imperfection and the self-bashing begins. What happens to your self-esteem then?

> *"It is impossible to live without*
> *failing at something,*
> *unless you live so cautiously*
> *that you might as well not have lived at all*
> *- in which case, you fail by default."*
> J. K. Rowling

Exercise - 48

Make a decision: Is this a good time to let go of your Self-Whip? If so, then take your Self-Whip and put it between any two pages in this book, or for that matter any book. You can even hide your whip behind the sofa or in your very own secret hiding place. Now you know where it is. Now you can retrieve it any time you wish to hurt yourself again. Reread the last sentence…why would we want to hurt ourselves? Write about your desire to hurt yourself.

> ***You might be a Chaos Person if...***
> your coworkers bought you a one-way ticket
> to a middle east country engaged in a civil war.

Going west from Baton Rouge, Louisiana on Interstate 10, the Mississippi River has an exit to Port Allen and Plaquemine. One day, I was traveling over this tall bridge heading for Plaquemine, Louisiana and was listening to the radio. Since I was not paying attention, I missed the exit!

The next exit was in Port Allen 2.5 miles from the bridge. My normal behavior was to beat myself up for being such an "idiot" and passing the exit. You see, when I judge myself, I then convict myself, and missing the exit is proof positive I am no good, a failure, and deserve to be condemned for life in the fiery pits of hell. After I convict myself, well, then I must punish the perpetrator of the crime: me. Can you hear my Self-Whip lashing?

Now, I have another coping skill and it works much better. This skill keeps my Self-Whip safely tucked away in my back pocket. When I now make a mistake, which I am prone to do, instead of the Self-Whip of condemnation, I tell myself, "Next time I'll do it differently." Isn't that much gentler than the abuse you normally inflict upon your wounded self?

When I play tennis, my habit was to berate myself, not my opponent, not my teammate. My displeasure was directed at me, right between my own eyes. Now when I miss a shot, I have a new coping skill. Whenever I berate myself aloud, I now apologize to myself; if I say it aloud, I apologize out loud. When my tennis mates hear me apologize to myself, they love my antics and jokingly shout, "Hay, David, how's that anger management book coming?"

Another coping skill I now employ after missing a shot is to coach myself to think of what I did wrong to miss an important stroke. I have become my coach instead of my angry parent expecting perfection. I cannot take back the missed opportunity to return the ball and maybe win the set, but I can learn from it, relax with the gentle (sometimes not so gentle) coaching and vow to do better. *Next time I'll do it differently.*

Exercise - 49

Would you care to use my wonderful, gentle coping skill, "Next time I'll do it differently?" Or do you wish to retrieve your Self-Whip and begin self-flagellating? Double check where you left it and you'll find it still there. Write a little about your self-abuse with your Self-Whip. Instead of self-flagellation, what can you do better next time?

You might be a Chaos Person if...
you are so full of guilt you feel so ashamed;
you just know it is you who is responsible
for Judas taking the silver.

Many people look to the past and bemoan their mistakes. Errors in judgment, behavior, hurting others, and the wrong decisions consume them now. It does not have to be that way, for recovering from a traumatic situation is all a matter of how we think about what happened. It is not so much about what happened to us, as what we make of the circumstance.

For example, Jerry Stovall and I discussed being fired. I was canned from my executive vice president job in 1982 and Jerry was let go in 1983 as the head football coach at Louisiana State University. He made a remarkable statement that has always stuck with me and when I've shared its wisdom, many people have been helped through their trying times of rejection and doubt.

He said, "David, I wouldn't hire anyone who had not been fired!" I looked at him incredulously and he continued, "I want to see if they are going to land on their feet or on their head!"

Depending on how you view any experience, you can turn your past stumbles into the fertilizer necessary for new growth. Are you a risk taker? Will you allow your mistakes to define you? Or use your regrets to change you for the better?

"Are you going to land on your feet or on your head?"

Exercise - 50

What is the opposite of love? Record it here and in the section entitled Life's Epilogue, you may find another point of view. At that time, you can compare your answer with another and perhaps stranger answer, one you had not yet thought about.

You might be a Chaos Person if...
you're so depressed,
even the Chaos Person jokes
fail to cheer you up.

Three Circle Model

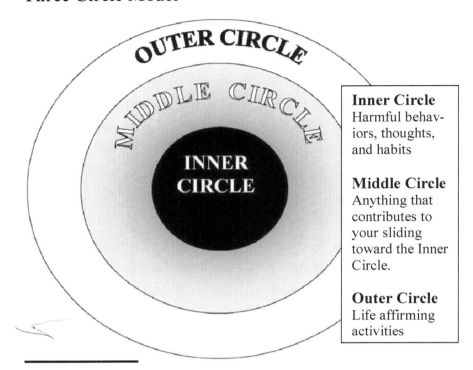

Inner Circle
Harmful behaviors, thoughts, and habits

Middle Circle
Anything that contributes to your sliding toward the Inner Circle.

Outer Circle
Life affirming activities

The Three Circle Model is three concentric circles, consisting of an inner, middle, and outer circle and each representing different behaviors, habits, and thoughts.

Inner Circle - This is what you recognized that is causing you dysfunction and needs to be changed. It could be behavior causing life-damaging consequences such as alcohol, drugs, compulsive gambling, sexually acting out, workaholics, religious addiction, or the enabling of others. Maybe it is hurting others or continuing love-limiting behaviors, dysfunctional family habits, unintentional hurting of others and behavior that is not life affirming or limits the flow of love. Continuing this behavior leads toward self-destructive consequences and problematic lifestyles.

Examples of what others have included in their *Inner Circles* are addictions, compulsions, dangerous, and/or destructive behavior, anything limiting the flow of love.

Middle Circle – These behaviors may not obviously belong in the *Inner Circle* but tend to make it easier to slide toward the *Inner Circle*. Items listed here are cautionary, slippery, or have a degree of uncertainty. Engaging in *Middle Circle* behavior does not mean failure; it represents the caution light warning us change is necessary.

Examples of what others have included in the *Middle Circle*: lonely, unmanaged anger, perfectionism, self-condemnation, emotionally drunk, unhealthy shame, living in extremes, ignoring or stuffing emotions, violating boundaries, allowing others to violate our boundaries, judgment, and black and white thinking.

Outer Circle - Healthy behaviors are leading away from what you listed in the *Inner Circle*. What belongs in the *Other Circle* is behavior that is healthy, safe, and beneficial to the fullest expression of love. Just practicing these behaviors is an act of self-love even if they are not done perfectly. Being gentle with yourself in this change process will help lead you toward the peace and serenity. *Outer Circle* items we want to develop, as habits are self-nurturing, create meaning, serenity, fulfillment, and joy.

Examples of *Outer Circle* are: enhanced life behaviors, connection to others, connection to ourselves, spiritual life, work, play, meditation, dancing, singing, living life to the fullest, honesty, recovery program, working, family, friendship, healthy sexual connection, affirming relationships, love, hobbies, friendships, etc. (see the expanded list in the Appendix entitled: List of Activities).

Exercise 51

List what you may think needs to be in your *Inner Circle*.

You might be a Chaos Person if...
you scrub the house from top to bottom
with a toothbrush because tomorrow,
the maid is coming.

In our headlong rush toward perfectionism, many people list all the items that they think belong here. Now go back and mark the 3 or 4 most destructive items you want to leave in your *Inner Circle*. List the remaining items as future considerations. You want to make progress, not be overwhelmed with the magnitude of *Inner Circle* items.

List what you may think needs to be in your *Middle Circle*. What is on your slippery slope threatening to wrap its long and slimy arms around you and suck you into the swamp of despair?

Make a gratitude list; what are you thankful for in your life?

From this gratitude list, you can now load your *Outer Circle*. What needs to be in your *Outer Circle*?

You might be a Chaos Person if...
your favorite picnic spot is the cemetery.

How many items do you have listed in your *Inner Circle*? Before you started doing *Thumb Work*, this is what took up a lot of your time and attention. Now that you are not doing the *Inner Circle* behaviors you need something to substitute for them. Think of some healthy behaviors you can do instead of destructive *Inner Circle* behaviors you know so well. It is recommended you have at least 2 or 3 *Outer Circle* behavior to compensate for every *Inner Circle* item listed. Check this ratio; do you have enough? If not, think up some more.

You might be a Chaos Person if...
your definition of a good marriage is,
"Ever third day, it isn't so bad."

Note: The Three Circle Model was developed by the men and women working a 12 Step Program in Sex Addicts Anonymous. Other twelve step programs are beginning to see the value in this tool

"I believe that every single event in life happens in a opportunity to choose love over fear."
Oprah Winfrey.

Conclusion

"In the end these things matter most:
How well did you love?
How fully did you live?
How deeply did you let go?"
Gautama Buddha

After reading these family dysfunctional habits, you may be understandably depressed. All families struggle with these habits; some do better than others do. No one grew up living in the sitcom representation of healthy families such as *Leave to Beaver, The Brady Bunch,* or *The Bill Cosby Show.* Since we now know these habits are silent killers of love, we can continue their use-or we can start violating them. We can become Family Rebels and change the hurtful patterns learned growing up. Remember…*love is not enough.*

You did not invent these family habits. Your family is like mine: for thousands and thousands of years our families have embraced a dysfunctional lifestyle, passing these habits on to subsequent generations. This was not done out of malice, spite, or hate, but what they knew best. As ineffective as these habits are, you never stopped to consider another way of loving.

Members of dysfunctional families who are working on changing by engaging in *Thumb Work* are not bad people trying to get good. We represent sick people who experience restrictive love from unhealthy coping skills, but who now want to find new and better methods to allow our great love to flow more freely without the associated pain. We did not invent these habits and restrictions, nor did we consciously learn them or purposely believe in them. We did not consciously pass them on to our kids.

No one escapes some degree of chaos for it is so ever prevalent; it is the human experience. This realization does not mean we can't improve. It does mean we can accept our state of chaos, lighten up on ourselves, have fun, and work on improving…we are a work in progress. Enjoy the journey.

You might be a Chaos Person if…
if you are human.

Now with this new awareness, we are attempting to find better ways of expressing the deep love burning in our hearts. Generations of dysfunctional families have been very successful at staying on these dysfunctional rails and enforcing and passing on these love-limiting habits. Because you are reading this book, you are already a change agent in your family. Your changing will seriously affect your life and make positive changes in the people you love.

What are humans meant to do; why are we here? Are we a mutation on the earth destroying its host? Are we a cancer destined to kill what supports us? I think not. So exploring this question is a powerful exercise in meaning; what is the meaning of human existence?

My father thought humans were here on earth to create something to build. After all he was an engineer and it is what engineers do, build things. His realization started my thought process and the conclusion I came to is a little different. I think life is a learning experience; we are here on earth to learn something. This was comforting to me for many years; recently I learned what it is we are supposed to learn.

Humans are born to learn how to **love**. Remember love is not enough; we have to learn how to give and receive healthy love. Most people do not know how to love as evidenced by these dysfunctional family habits. However, by knowing these unhealthy habits and then learning new ways to express yourself profoundly increases the effectiveness of your love. New healthy habits allow love to flow freely, the people around you know it, you feel it, and when what used to cause great pain becomes a source of comfort…you now know a better way of loving.

The changes you accomplish will have a cataclysmic ripple effect. These changes will allow you to start feeling better about yourself; changing from self-loathing to self-love. Your peace and serenity will grow, magnify, and become a new way of living. Change is possible. We do not have to teach the next generation our dysfunction that in turn will teach the next generation this chaos. Together, we can change family history.

"We are here to laugh at the odds and live our lives
so well that Death will tremble to take us."
Charles Bukowski

Lighting up the World

I saw an internet video clip about a fashion photographer, Rick Guidotti. In this clip, Guidotti talks about his former photography subjects as being high-end fashion models sashaying down the runway. Now he takes images of people with medical conditions.

What is striking about his current photographs is that instead of the usual medical textbook images depicting people with deformities as being gross, abnormal, and ugly, he captures their beauty. He views them as beautiful, his camera captures what he now sees, and the change is a striking transformation.

Rick says he "...now interprets beauty differently." Medical textbooks capture their deformity but "misses their humanity...this is sad." Rick wants us to "...celebrate all differences" to see what is there "...their gorgeousness." One mother said about the photographs Rich did of her child with a medical condition, "I suddenly saw a picture of my child the way I saw him..." not the "...way others view him." Rick wants the world not to see the diagnosis but a human being, "...not a *what but a who*." Rick thinks the world has a "...set idea of beauty," and he wants us to see, "...beauty differently."

What Rick does through his photographic eye and records on cellulose is letting go what is not there and capturing what is there. He lets go of his preconceived definitions and trains his eyes to see the image differently.

One Sunday, I looked at a large woman, not attractive by the world's standards, and mentally let go all the usual definitions, such as, large, female, elderly, wrinkled, and started connecting with her on a different plane. I forced my eyes to see her beauty; I wanted the image to be one of Rick's photographs, one not distorted by other's definitions. Doing this brief exercise, I felt my barriers to this woman melt and I then felt an overwhelming desire to send love to her. I did and it felt grand.

The key problem I encounter when working with wounded, depressed, and unhappy people is a lack of connection...starting from a disconnection from themselves and then with others. This is why love often becomes so distorted and destructive. When people experience a disconnection from themselves, they feel it but do not realize the problem. Without this awareness, they develop an obsessive need to connect to someone, somewhere, some way. With this ardent need, they latch upon another or group in order to feel connected. If this connection is threatened and is the only place they feel connected, most will do most anything to keep this connection alive including hanging on to a toxic relationship. Statistically, a battered woman will leave her relationship and return thirteen times before she can leave for good. Many wounded people are so desperate they hang on to hurtful people, bond with gangs, or join cults; anything not to feel disconnected. Think of a teenage boy when offered a joint of marijuana by a friend. He feels so disconnected from himself (remember yourself as an adolescent), his peers become his value system and so he takes his first hit, often contrary to the basic morals taught in his family.

Consider letting go of the barriers between yourself and others, let go of the definition our culture has inflicted upon us and allow the best part of ourselves to connect with others. Allow yourself to connect in a deeper and more profound way.

When Rick talks about humanity, about what he now sees in his subjects, his face lights up with joy. With this new awareness, he is now free to express the profound love in his heart, the same love in your heart screaming to be free of restrictions, limitations, conventions, and definitions of who is okay and who is not okay to love. Freeing others from the prison of definition also releases us to be connected…we now are free. And in this state…*love is enough.*

Exercise 52

Watch a clip of Rich Guidotti.

http://www.youtube.com/watch?v=USECdjN7Siw

In a public place, practice seeing others without any limitation or definition. Let go and allow your love to extend to another by thinking about them without the normal barriers of definitions; you both will be richer from the experience.

Life's Epilogue

What is the opposite of love? Many say it is hate, some say indifference and some say contempt. Although all of these definitions have merit, maybe the opposite of love is something much different.

On October 17, 1992, two Baton Rouge teenage boys, Yoshihiro Hattori and Webb Haymaker, were excited about the Halloween party they planned to attend that evening. Yoshihiro was an exchange student from Nagoya, Japan and the Haymakers were his host family during his stay. Yoshihiro dressed in a suit like his movie idol, John Travolta, from the movie *Saturday Night Fever*. This was to be Yoshi's first Halloween party and Webb wanted to show his Japanese friend the American custom of Halloween. Unfortunately, the boys mistakenly went to the wrong house.

The boys walked up on the carport of the Rodney Peairs' house and rang the doorbell on the carport door. They waited a few moments and when no one answered the door, they turned around and walked back toward their car. Suddenly, Rodney Peairs came out of his back door and yelled, "Freeze!" In his hands was a loaded .44 Magnum handgun pointed at the boys.

Yoshihiro Hattori did not know the meaning of "Freeze" and probably thought he had said, "Please" for he started walking toward Mr. Peairs saying, "We're here for the party." When Webb saw the gun, he yelled at his friend to stop but at that same moment, Peairs fired his handgun point bank at Yoshi. The bullet entered his left lung and excited near the 7th rib. In a foreign land on a cold concrete driveway, Yoshi bled to death in Webb's arms as he tried to comfort his dying friend. As Yoshi was dying on his carport, Mr. Peairs immediately went back into his house. Yoshi had been in this country 60 days.

Mr. Peairs was tried for manslaughter and at the trial his wife, Bonnie, testified, "He was coming real fast…" so she told her husband, "…to get the gun." Bonnie continued her testimony, "There was no thinking involved. I wish I could have thought. If I could have just thought." How does a 6'2'' adult man armed with a large caliber weapon mistake a small 16-year-old kid dressed in a white boogie suit and showing no sign of being violent as someone who is a serious threat? What was Peairs afraid of? All of Peairs' guns were legally obtained and licensed; he was on his own property. The law could not fault him here. However, even though Yoshi made no threatening moves, Mr, Peairs leveled a very powerful gun at the boy and fired. The district attorney summed up the situation to the jury: "It started with the ringing of the doorbell. No masks, no disguises." The two young people "…ringing doorbells are not attempting to make unlawful entry. They didn't walk to the back yard; they didn't start peeking in the windows."

A Baton Rouge jury acquitted Mr. Peairs of manslaughter, shocking many who followed the trial and causing much disbelief in Japan. This tragic event created an international incident with both high level US and Japanese elected officials entered the story, ultimately triggering a push for greater gun control. After the shooting, one million Americans and 1.65 million Japanese signed a petition urging stronger gun controls in the U.S. They presented this petition to Ambassador Walter Mondale on November 22, 1993, who delivered it to President Bill Clinton. Shortly thereafter, on December 3, 1993, the Brady Bill passed; Mondale presented Hattori's parents with a copy.

Mr. Peairs was later tried in civil court where he was found negligent and the parents of Yoshihiro Hattori received a $685,000 settlement. The Hattori family used this money to create scholarships for other exchange students and the rest they donated toward the gun control efforts in this country.

At Yoshi's memorial service in the Unitarian Church, Reverend Steve Crumb echoed the thoughts of all those present at this service: "How could this happen?" In his remarks, Crumb reflected upon the availability of guns and the fear of others having guns creating an environment of fear. His response to this question was an even more important question to ask, "How could it not happen?"

The Hattori family later donated two large stones to this country as a memorial for their beloved son. They now rest on the grounds of the Baton Rouge Unitarian Church where they hold a special place in the hearts and minds of all people dedicated to a peaceful world. The stones now have names, commemorative titles befitting the violence and tragedy that brought them here from the quarries of Nagoya, Japan. One stone is called *Fear Less* and the other is *Love More*.

You still may be wondering about the opening question, "What is the opposite of love?" The opposite of love is not hate, indifference, or contempt, although all are obvious manifestations of the lack of love. The opposite of love is *fear*.

Many of the habits dysfunctional families use are not from the lack of love but are the result of fear. Knowing the love-limiting habits and behaviors of dysfunctional families is a wonderful beginning to lower the fear, allowing us to be real, allowing us all to learn how to love better.

Yoshihiro Hattori will not have died in vain if we learn this lesson. In order to express the profound feelings of love deep within us, we have to *fear* less and *love* more.

Love is not enough

"...but for my own part,
if a book is well written,
I always find it too short."
Jane Austen

It is my fervent hope...
you have found this book
...*too short*.

Appendix

Declaration from Dependency

I started this change process in August of 1987 when I admitted my son to addiction rehabilitation at Charter Hospital in Kingwood, Texas. Many months later, I decided that what I needed were goals for me to accomplish (*Thumb Work*). These goals were not a New Year's resolution to be made and then forgotten in the chaos of life. This was a declaration about a profound revolution in my life. I was tired of hurting so badly and causing the people I loved so much pain. Therefore, on December 8, 1988, I wrote my *Declaration of Dependency*.

I had not yet achieved many of these goals when I wrote this statement, although progress was being made. After putting these goals on paper, my *Declaration from Dependency* became my road map for my new life, what I wanted to accomplish before they threw dirt over my grave. I am so glad I did. Maybe this exercise will inspire you to make your own statement of how you want to live the rest of your life.

Declaration from Dependency

> *I, David W. Earle, hereby declare: henceforth, I will no longer be the doormat of the human race. I make this proclamation as my Declaration from Dependency. I will lovingly confront any, and all, people who I feel psychologically dependent upon and exercise my options in that relationship for my own interdependence.*
>
> *I will create a personal atmosphere of interdependence, striving always to consider what David wants and needs. Having that knowledge, I now know if I choose to deviate from those wants/needs a price will require a payment. However, I will not make this choice out of my sick abandonment needs and I alone will decide if David is willing to pay the price.*
>
> *I will not give to others the authorization, expressed or implied, to control any part of my life. I will live my life*

in a manner not requiring others to control or take responsibility for my life and/or actions. I will steadfastly resist any efforts by others to control me. Instead of allowing my fear of being controlled, this goal is achieved by the open and honest realization and proclamation of what is right for David.

I will, henceforth, allow other people to be responsible for their own feelings as I will be completely responsible for mine.

I will relate to others in a healthier manner, not seeking their approval by striving to please them, and losing my identity in the process. On every decision I will ask myself, "What are David's wants and needs?" the answer to this question will be considered first, not last. My personal needs / wants will guide my every response, every action, and in every relationship. Nor will I allow these actions to become selfish but rather a function of self-care.

I will not attempt to influence or manipulate other people to care for me by acting out my family role as the mascot or clown. I will not give in to my compulsive drive to be the center of attention in order to fill my burning desire for acceptance. I will no longer give up my own personal identity in the pursuit of this incisive need for acceptance. This sacrifice of self was in order for me to receive the personal attention I demanded to fill my hole of isolation and abandonment fears.

The fear that others may not accept me, may not love me for the way I really am is invalid and I no longer will operate under that premise. In addition, I will not for the sake of this commitment, give up my God-given sense of humor but will strive for balance.

My personal identity is of far greater value then my need to fill this hole in my soul with the lives of other people, material possessions, status, or mind-altering chemicals. I will constantly find good self-talk messages to give myself reinforcing my basic goodness and I will find many good things I like about myself and compliment myself upon those qualities. I will not scold myself for tasks not accomplished; mistakes made; or from the rejection by others; these will not control my happiness anymore.

I will be constantly remind myself my worth as a human is from my higher power which has already been calculated by a divine and benevolent God. Anything I say, or do, or accomplish, is after that self-worth calculation and cannot be added to nor detracted from my already established unit of self-worth.

A perfect Creator created me; therefore, I am perfect. The spark of the divine lives within me and I can and will fill any empty holes in my soul with the God, my higher power. I will henceforth, allow this God-part of my soul to reveal to me my own self-worth, expand my self-love, and create my own self-fulfillment from within me.

I hereby declare that on this date, December 8, 1988 that I, David W. Earle will no longer require outside things, people, mood-altering events, excitement, and substances to fill any part of my soul/self. Henceforth, I will inwardly seek solutions to all fears, incompleteness, emptiness, abandonment, hurt, and shame. I now know, my answers are to be found within myself where me, myself, and I now live in that special place with my higher power in serenity and love.

These lofty goals declared in 1988 have come true for me. Somehow declaring something, putting it on paper and facing the source of the greatest amount of pain developed strength more powerful than if I had not declared them and just thought about what I wanted.

These declarations then became my vision statement, my touchstone. Over the years as I read them again, I realized, yes, I was on the right track. If you think my declaration statement will help you achieve your goals, you are welcome to use any or all of it. I hope this example helps you achieve your goals.

You might be a Chaos Person if...
you are drowning and someone else's life flashes before your eyes.

Weekly Progress Report – Example

	Questionable Coping Skills		Positive Coping Skills	
Don't	Frightened of angry people		Overcoming the fear	
Talk	Not communicating honestly		Say what needs to be said with respect	
	Worrying -how others may think		Being be the person you truly are	
	Protecting family secrets		Share your pain with safe people	
	Projecting false okayness		Be real – let go of falseness	
Don't	Isolating, hiding, not honest		Increase your willingness to trust	
Trust	Hiding behind a mask		Be real	
	Distrust of others		Trusting those worthy of your trust	
	Distrust of yourself		Self-trust	
	Lack of connection with others		Reach out and connect	
	Lying		Be faithful to the truth	
Don't	Not expressing your emotions		Use the Mood Chart	
Feel	Shut down emotions (stuffing)		Use the Mood Chart	
	Emotionally numb/ drunk		Use the Mood Chart	
Don't	Unwillingness to change		Know changing toward peace is okay	
Change	Allow fear to control behavior		Stand up for what is right	
	Rigid definition / role enforcement		Let go of rigid self-definition	
	Distortion between pain and love		Know love and pain are not the same	
Don't	Over / Under responsible		Decrease extremes	
Be Real	Over Focus on others		Self-care	
	Others responsible - my happiness		Take responsibility for your happiness	
	Victim role		Choose not to think/act like a victim	
	Focusing on other's defects		*Thumb work-* Focus on changing you	
Don't	Accepting personal criticism		You can hear criticism and still be okay	
Respect	Uncertain of boundaries		Know your boundaries	
Boundaries	Wishy-washy personal boundaries		Assertively defend your boundaries	
	Rescuing - owning others problems		Allowing natural consequences	
	Feel guilty when assertive		It is okay to stand up for yourself	
Don't	Taking other's inventory		Take your own moral inventory	
Accept	Low self-worth		Believe in yourself	
	Black/white thinking		Acceptance	
	Blaming (judgment)		Allow others to be themselves	
	Fear of people and authority figures		You are okay	
	Lack of spontaneity		Have fun- *Choose to be happy*	
	People pleasing/approval		You are okay as you are	

In the first blank column, rate yourself from 1 to 5 with 5 being the most severe. Compare your progress each week you post in the second blank column. Where have you improved and what still needs work? This is a sample of what you may or may not be working on; customize it for yourself.

You might be a Chaos Person if....
you got kicked out of the airport for
leaving your emotional baggage unattended.

Suggested Reading

> *"Owning our story and loving ourselves*
> *through that process is the bravest*
> *thing we will ever do."*
> Anonymous

7 Habits of Highly Effective People - Stephen R. Covey

Anger - Thich Nhat Hanh

Another Chance - Sharon -Cruse

Beyond the Relaxation Response - Hebert Benson. M.D.

Big Book of Alcoholics Anonymous - Bill Wilson

Calling All Women - Sharon Wegscheider-Cruse

Codependency No More - Melody Beattie

Daily Reflections for Highly Effective People - Stephen R. Covey

Getting to Yes - William L Ury, Roger Fister, Bruce M. Patton

I'm Ok – You're Ok - Thomas A. Harros, M.D.

Just Listen - Mark Goulston

Learning to Love Yourself - Sharon Wegscheider-Cruse

Life After Divorce - Sharon Wegscheider-Cruse

Love - Leo Buscaglia

Man's Search for Meaning - Viktor E. Frankl

The Magic of Conflict - Thomas F. Crum

The Power of Now - Eckhart Tolle

The Seven Spiritual Laws of Success - Deepak Chopra

The Way of the Wizard - Deepak Chopra

Understanding Co-Dependency - Sharon -Cruse

Circumplex Model for Marriage & Families – Dr. David Oleson

Wake UP! - Tom Owen-Towle

> *"Books may well be the only true magic."*
> Alice Hoffman

*"There are two basic motivating forces: fear and love.
When we are afraid, we pull back from life.
When we are in love, we open to all that life has to offer
with passion, excitement, and acceptance."*
John Lennon

*"A miracle is a shift in perception
from fear to love."*
Marianne Williamson

*"Love is what we are born with.
Fear is what we learned here."*
Marianne Williamson

*"Wicked men obey from fear;
good men, from Love."*
Aristotle

*"Fear isn't the opposite of love,
fear is what arises when love isn't there,
so maybe, I reason, there is only one emotion.
There is only love, and the absence of love."*
Anna Raverat

"Love does not hurt people, fear does."
Jeff Erno

*"Fear shoves you from behind;
love beckons you forward."*
P. A. Monson

*"No one wants their life thrown into chaos.
That is why a lot of people keep that
threat under control, and are somehow
capable of sustaining a house or a
structure that is already rotten.
They are the engineers of the superseded."*
Paulo Coelho

*"The mind is everything.
What you think you will become."*
Buddha

About the Author

David W. Earle, LPC combines his counseling skills with his twenty-plus-years of executive management experience into a powerful matrix called Business Coaching. Using this technique, Earle assists leaders in increasing their leadership effectiveness through gaining new people skills. He is also a teacher, trainer, author, counselor, and alternative dispute professional.

Earle earned a Master's of Science from Texas A&M and has held executive management positions in various fields including industrial construction, private investment banking, and corporate trouble shooting. He is now the president of the Earle Company, an organization dedicated to change.

He has published five other books: *What To Do While You Count To 10* (management of strong emotions), *Professor of Pain* (a lesson before living), *Iron Mask* (peace is your birthright), *Red Roses 'n Pinstripes* (despair to meaning), and *Gilligan's Notes* (communication skills). Other self-help books are *The Wisdom of the Twelve Steps*. This is a set of workbooks specifically designed to help people in recovery work through the Twelve Steps. He has also co-authored two books on leadership: *Leadership-Helping Others Succeed* and *Extreme Leadership*. His blog is: *Lessons in Living*. All of these are all self-help books designed to inspire as well as inform.

Earle has been on the panel as a mediator and/or arbitrator for various organizations such as U.S. Federal Court-Middle District, Equal Employment Opportunity Commission (EEOC), Financial Industry Regulator Authority (FINRA), Natural Futures Association (NFA), Federal Deposit Insurance Corporation (FDIC), and the Louisiana Supreme Court. He was also on the faculty of the University of Phoenix for over 10 years.

His trademarked motto is *My Life Will Change When I Change*™; he enjoys tennis and he lives in Baton Rouge with his wife, Penny, and their dog and cat, Fletcher and Hobbes.

You can contact him at lessonsbeforeliving@gmail.com

Outer Circle Activities - sample

Aerobics
Aircraft spotting
Airsoft
Altar art
Animal rescue
Animation
Antique cars
Antiques
Archery
Arts and crafts
Artwork
Astronomy
Astrophotography
Auto detailing
Autocross
Autographs
Aviation
Backgammon
Backpacking
Badminton
Baking
Barbecue
Baseball cards
Beading
Beekeeping
Birdwatching
Blacksmithing
Blogging
Board games
Bonsai
Books
Bottles
Bowling
Boxing
Bridge
Butterflies
Cake making
Calendars
Calligraphy
Cameras
Camping
Candlesticks
Canoeing
Cans
Card games
Caving
Checkers
Cheerleading
Chemistry
Chess
Chinese Checkers
Circuit bending
Climbing

Comic books
Computer graphics
Computers
Conifer cones
Cribbage
Cricket
Crochet
Cross country
Cross-stitch
Crystals
Cue sports
Currency
Cycling
cycling
Dancing
Dancing
Darkroom
Dice
Die-cast toys
Diving
Dog training
Dollhouses
Dominoes
Drawing
Dumpster diving
Electronic circuits
Electronics
Elephant training
Embroidery
Enamels
Engraving
Enthusiasm
Facebooking
Falconry
Fashion Design
Fencing
Figure painting
Film-making
Fishing
Fish keeping
Football
Fossils
Fountain pens
Friends
Gamebook
Gardening
Gardening
Genealogy
German board

Grafting
Guns
Gymnastics
Handbags
Hardware hacking
Hats
Hearts
Henna
Herpetoculture
Hiking
Historical reenactment
Home Canning
Home Repairs
Horoscopes
Horse riding
Horseshoes
House making
Human agility
Hunting
Ice Skating
Image editing
Interior Design
Internet-based hobbies
Jewelry
Jogging
Jousting
Juggling
Karaoke
Keychains
Kite flying
Knitting
Knives
Lacrosse
Lasers
Leather crafting
LEGO
Letterboxing
License Plates
Literature
Magic tricks
Marbles
Martial arts
Militaries
Miniature figures
Model aircraft
Model cars
Model military vehicles
Model railways
Monopoly

Music
MySpace
Netball
News
Newsgroups
Observation
Off-roading
Origami
Outdoor
Paintball
Painting
Papercraft
Patches
Pente
People watching
Performing arts
Photography
Physics
Plates
Plinking
Poetry
Poker
Postcards
Posters
Pottery
Quilting
Quotations
Racquetball
Radio
Radio control toys
Rafting
Rallying
Random surfing
Reading
Recordings
Refurbishing
Renaissance
Robots
Rock climbing
Rock hounding
Rook
Rowing
Sailing
Scrabble
Scrapbooking
SCUBA diving
Sculpture
Sewing
Shooting
Shopping
Singing
Skateboarding

Soapmaking
Soccer
Songwriting
Souvenirs
Spades
Spoons
Sports
Spud gun
Squash
Stained glass
Stamping
Stamps
Stickers
Stone skipping
Storytelling
Stumbling
Upon
Sudoku
Surfing
Swimming
Swords
Table tennis
Tae Kwon Do
Teddy bears
Tennis
Theater
Thimbles
Tiddlywinks
Tole painting
Toys
Trading Cards
Train spotting
Trampoline
Traveling
Treasure hunting
Trolling
Unicycle
Urban Exploration
Video games
Videogames
Volleyball
Walking
War reenactment
Watches and Clocks
Watercolor
Weaving
Weight lifting
Wine tasting
Wood carving
Woodworking
World War II
Writing

Acknowledgements

Someone once said, "No one reads acknowledgements." Perhaps they should have said, "Acknowledgements are only read by those who should be included, by those who hope to be included but are unsure if they are, and those who should be, but are overlooked and put the book down with understandably hurt feelings." For anyone I left out from this list, please accept my apologies, it was not my intention.

Most books would not have been completed except by the strength of encouragement of others and *Love is Not Enough* is no exception. All authors face the **Dragon of Doubt** for writing is an exposure of the author's soft underbelly to the intimacy of other's truth, perception, and judgment. These comments can tickle, coddle, satisfy, encourage, or frighten tender author's feelings. This author is the *tenderest* of the tender. Well-deserved criticism is valuable but still often painful. For every negative criticism, I need many positive ones to keep me pointed in the right direction. I am thankful for this support of others and…gulp…I am grateful for those comments that hurt, but that I need to hear.

I read the book *Wake Up* on a weekend retreat and was so impressed I requested the author, Tom Oeen-Towle's permission to include a quote him when I wrote *Professor of Pain*. Since that contact, he has sent me little notes of encouragement and his is one of the voices keeping the dragons away.

I asked several friends to review this book and Melinda George told me it was "…therapy on pages." In Charles Cruthirds' review, he said he hesitated…"to use the word book because it transcends that-- it is at once engaging, thought-provoking, but most of all, HONEST." Jan Zeringue said the title was profound and her valuable insight added much need wisdom and to others over the years.

What I did not expect and what amazed me about Charles, Melinda, and Jan's feedback, is that they all worked the exercises. Charles said, "…I wanted to…throw the book across the room on a few occasions…sometimes the truth hurts…" Jan said, "…you gave me some routes for growth" and Melinda said, "It helped me …to locate myself and find answers for WHY." I think these friends of mine may have experienced a little "unlearning".

I had the benefit of five editors, Laci Talley, Cliff Carle, ~~and~~ Lee Tyler Williams and Sm Sublett. Laci's quiet demand for honesty and insistence on hearing my author's voice kept me from chasing rabbits down dark alleys of insecurity. This is the last book she committed to edit for me, as she wants to put more time into her own writing. Keep a lookout for her work, as I know it will be terrific. Lee joined the team late and worked on some last minute changes to the original proof such as this acknowledgement.

I call Cliff Carle the *Sherlock Homes of Editing*. After reading some of the Chaos jokes, he suggested we collaborate and write a joke book entitled: *You might need a therapist if...* Cliff was my editor for *What To Do While You Count To 10* as well as this one so I already experienced his serious side. I look forward to laughing with him as we share the humor of therapy. Sam Sublett made all previous editing better.

Dr. David H. Olson, a professor of the University of Minnesota not only agreed to allow the inclusion of the *Circumplex Model of Family Systems,* and gave several coaching sessions on how to best to express it. I told him after I received his suggestions that it felt as if I was back in graduate school, working on my thesis.

My acknowledgements cannot be complete without thanking my partner in all my writings, Penny Earle, my bride of over twenty years. She thinks I have a valuable message and is willing to review what I write, often catching what previous editors missed. As the fifth editor, she sometimes laughs at my spelling, chokes on my syntax, and is repelled at my sentence structure but her red pen always insures me that she sees our work as valuable, and I feel her love. What else is there?

> *"Be thankful for what you have;*
> *you'll end up having more. If you concentrate*
> *on what you don't have,*
> *you will never, ever have enough."*
> Oprah Winfrey

When we finally freed ourselves from the burden
of years of encrusted dysfunctional family rules
and step into the light of acceptance...

Love is certainly enough.

Disclaimer

All the lessons and coping skills presented in ***Love is Not Enough*** are the best thinking of the author, my husband. These are his realities, his best learning from living many years in chaos, causing himself and others considerable pain and suffering. Here is the wisdom he collected by changing his life. Yes, he does his own ***thumb work***.

Having thoroughly edited this book, I know what is collected between its covers and it is true for me. However, the truth and what he practices are sometimes at odds; I know him well.

I love him for his attempts at making our lives better. I see him struggle with his own chaos habits sometimes coming directly at me affecting my day. I respect his willingness, sometime begrudgingly, to hear how his behavior affected me.

Using the principles found in this book has made our lives so much better, but you need to know…your self-help guru, my husband is definitely *not perfect*.

Penny Earle

Made in the USA
Charleston, SC
04 December 2014